Canoeing and Kayaking
for People With Disabilities

American Canoe Association

Janet A. Zeller

Author

Human Kinetics

Library of Congress Cataloging-in-Publication Data

Zeller, Janet.
   Canoeing and kayaking for people with disabilities / Janet A. Zeller.
     p. cm.
   Includes bibliographical references and index.
   ISBN-13: 978-0-7360-8674-5
   ISBN-10: 0-7360-8674-9
   ISBN-13: 978-0-7360-8329-4 (soft cover)
   ISBN-10: 0-7360-8329-4 (soft cover)
  1.   Canoeing for people with disabilities--Study and teaching--Handbooks, manuals, etc. 2. Kayaking for people with disabilities--Study and teaching--Handbooks, manuals, etc. I. Title.
   GV777.58.Z45 2009
   797.122087--dc22

2009010060

ISBN-10: 0-7360-8329-4 (print)   ISBN-10: 0-7360-8674-9 (Adobe PDF)
ISBN-13: 978-0-7360-8329-4 (print)   ISBN-13: 978-0-7360-8674-5 (Adobe PDF)

This book is a revised edition of *Canoeing and Kayaking for Persons with Physical Disabilities: Instruction Manual,* written by Anne Wortham Webre and Janet Zeller, and published in 1990 by the American Canoe Association.

The Web addresses cited in this text were current as of February 18, 2009, unless otherwise noted.

Content Editor: Laurie Gullion; **Acquisitions Editor:** Gayle Kassing, PhD; **Developmental Editor:** Melissa Feld; **Assistant Editor:** Rachel Brito; **Copyeditor:** Patsy Fortney; **Proofreader:** Anne Rogers; **Indexer:** Craig Brown; **Permission Manager:** Dalene Reeder; **Graphic Designer:** Nancy Rasmus; **Graphic Artist:** Yvonne Griffith; **Cover Designer** Keith Blomberg; **Photographer (cover):** Photo courtesy of Karen Schlicher; **Photographer (interior):** © Human Kinetics unless otherwise noted; **Photo Production Manager:** Jason Allen; **Art Manager:** Kelly Hendren; **Associate Art Manager:** Alan L. Wilborn; **Illustrator:** Gary Hunt, except illustrations on pages 34-35 courtesy of the National Safe Boating Council; **Printer:** Versa Press

Cover photo: Paddling for all in Big Bay, Michigan: two of the paddlers have a disability.

Printed in the United States of America   10 9 8 7 6 5 4 3 2 1

The paper in this book is certified under a sustainable forestry program.

Human Kinetics
Web site: www.HumanKinetics.com

United States: Human Kinetics
P.O. Box 5076
Champaign, IL 61825-5076
800-747-4457
e-mail: humank@hkusa.com

Canada: Human Kinetics
475 Devonshire Road Unit 100
Windsor, ON N8Y 2L5
800-465-7301 (in Canada only)
e-mail: info@hkcanada.com

Europe: Human Kinetics
107 Bradford Road
Stanningley
Leeds LS28 6AT, United Kingdom
+44 (0) 113 255 5665
e-mail: hk@hkeurope.com

Australia: Human Kinetics
57A Price Avenue
Lower Mitcham, South Australia 5062
08 8372 0999
e-mail: info@hkaustralia.com

New Zealand: Human Kinetics
Division of Sports Distributors NZ Ltd.
P.O. Box 300 226 Albany
North Shore City
Auckland
0064 9 448 1207
e-mail: info@humankinetics.co.nz

Contents

Preface

Welcome! By selecting this book, you have shown you are interested in opening the world of paddling to someone who has a disability. That person may be your student, a family member, a friend, or perhaps yourself after a disability has became part of your life.

This book is designed as a resource guide for paddling instructors, individuals who have disabilities, recreation program providers, and health care professionals who want to share the sport with people who have disabilities. The emphasis is on safety and integration with how-to guidance on adaptation development, techniques, equipment, and resources.

The goal of this guidebook is to increase integrated paddling opportunities for people who have disabilities. Together, all paddlers can experience the challenge, discovery, beauty, renewal, and freedom that paddling opportunities provide. In addition, through the shared experience of paddling, people with and without disabilities can get to know each other as individuals and move beyond the barriers of uncertainty and misunderstanding often created by disability.

Although this guidebook is packed with information, it is not a detailed guide to all aspects of paddling. It is intended to supplement the technical information found in the American Canoe Association's (ACA) endorsed manuals, instructional resources on the ACA Web site at www.americancanoc.org, and the resources listed in appendix A.

Reading a manual should not be a substitute for paddling instruction or for instructor training for those who teach others. Instructor certification is evidence of paddling and rescue skills, experience teaching paddling, technical knowledge, and group management and safety awareness. When selecting an instructor, ask if candidates are certified and who granted the certification. Contact the ACA National Office for information about certified ACA instructors in your area and about those who have additional training working with paddlers who have disabilities through the completion of an Adaptive Paddling Workshop.

Adaptive paddling has evolved since the 1990 publication of *Canoeing and Kayaking for Persons with Physical Disabilities: An Instruction Manual* by Anne Webre and Janet Zeller. Although this revised guidebook covers the basics of adaptive paddling, it also conveys the knowledge and best practices developed in more recent years by instructors, paddlers, and recreation and health care providers. This knowledge will continue to grow through a continued sharing of information. We are always open to new ideas and welcome additional adaptations and techniques that have proven successful. What works for one paddler may be just the technique another paddler needs.

Please share what you have discovered with others by sending an e-mail about a new adaptation, technique, or tip you learned to Adaptive Paddling on the American Canoe Association Web site at sei@americancanoe.org. Also, you are invited to send your specific questions to the Web site, and experienced adaptive paddling instructors will respond to you.

Acknowledgments

Paddling is a gift to the spirit and a joy we pass on to others. This book is dedicated to all who work so hard to introduce others to the world of paddling. It is also written in recognition of those who have given so much to the development of adaptive paddling. Thanks to Annie Wortham Webre, who shared my belief in 1990 that until we could write down some instructions and get them into the hands of others, the premise that people who have disabilities can safely paddle would not be fully recognized. It is because of our book *Canoeing and Kayaking for Persons With Physical Disabilities* that adaptive paddling has grown in several countries.

Thanks to Colin Twitchell as well. He is the other pillar of adaptive paddling and the guru behind so much of the development in adaptive seating and paddlegrips taking place in the market today. His dedication and hundreds of volunteer hours resulted in the principles, processes, and equipment design that moved the sport forward; now Scott LeBlanc is assuming that role in working with other adaptive equipment leaders. Annie and Colin also worked with me in developing the first Adaptive Paddling Workshop (APW) in 1990. The progress that has been made since that time would not have been possible without Annie and Colin's groundwork.

The American Canoe Association must also be recognized and thanked. From 1989 when I first presented to the ACA board of directors the need to integrate paddlers with disabilities into the sport, they embraced my vision and made a place at the ACA table for adaptive paddling. Over the years as the APWs have expanded across the country, the number of instructors committed to integrating all paddlers safely into the sport has grown. Thanks to the hundreds who have completed APWs and have gone on to spread the joy of paddling. The continuing growth of knowledge, training, and opportunities in adaptive paddling would not have been possible without the long-term commitment and hard work of the cadre of ACA Adaptive Paddling Workshops and adaptive paddling equipment instructors across the country. This book is dedicated to you all.

Good paddling!

Janet Zeller

Introduction

In 2008 one of every five people in the United States had a disability, making people with disabilities the largest minority in the country (National Organization on Disability, 2007). Given those high and increasing numbers, it's likely that disability affects your life in some way, either personally or through the life of a friend or family member.

Who Has a Disability?

According to the Americans with Disabilities Act (ADA), the legal definition of disability is a physical or mental impairment that substantially limits one or more of a person's major life activities, such as walking, seeing, hearing, breathing, thinking, or caring for one's self. According to the University of California at San Francisco's Disability Statistics Center, only 1.7 million people with disabilities, or 8 percent of this population, use wheelchairs, crutches, walkers, or other mobility devices. The vast majority of disabilities are not obvious.

In America we are an aging population. In 2008 the U.S. Census Bureau estimated that by 2030, more than 70 million Americans will be over 65. Disability often comes with aging, and the unavoidable truth is that if you live long enough, you will likely experience some level of disability. Despite the passage of years and the resulting changes in our bodies, many of us want to continue to recreate. Paddling is a low-impact sport, both on the body and on the environment, so it fits well into our changing lifestyles.

Whether disability has changed a person's life suddenly or activities have become more difficult gradually, the great news is that the person may still be able to paddle. Making paddling available to a person who has a disability requires information about safe adaptations and techniques along with integrated opportunities, in which paddlers who have disabilities are accepted without question. This guidebook is designed as a resource to make that paddling a reality.

Why Canoeing or Kayaking?

Paddling provides many unique opportunities. Gliding freely across the surface of the water, experiencing wildlife, mastering new skills, exercising for good health, choosing one's own limits, and recreating with friends are some of the best reasons for canoeing or kayaking. Paddlers can enjoy the experience from the first paddle stroke, and fulfillment is found at all skill levels.

The participant decides which type of paddling to pursue, with choices ranging from a quiet paddle on a calm lake to the challenge of a whitewater river, touring by sea kayak, or competition at special events. New challenges are always available. A person needs to be willing to accept instruction, be challenged, and adjust to new situations.

Canoeing and kayaking are activities that emphasize ability. Skill is determined by ability and attitude, whether or not the paddler has a disability. The freedom offered by paddling pushes aside the barriers presented by disabilities. A body that may be uncooperative on land becomes part of a sleek craft gliding through the water. Together, paddlers with and without disabilities can share all aspects of the sport. Water is the ultimate equalizer.

This guidebook contains unique information needed by instructors, paddlers, therapists, and recreation providers in order to open paddling to individuals who have disabilities. It also describes adaptations to manage the impact of paddlers' disabilities and to focus on their abilities.

The emphasis in instruction should always be on the ability of the paddler within the limits of the disability. This emphasis is not difficult to achieve with the right tools. This guidebook is a toolbox of information and suggestions to help the instructor and paddler work together effectively.

First, use the guidebook's basic tools to create the framework for effective instruction: the general guidelines, risk management, evaluation, the legal requirements, checklists, evaluation of students' abilities, the paddler's interview, and the possible implications for paddling of the disabilities involved. Then use the finishing tools including adaptations, additional techniques for rescues and rolls, equipment suggestions, and other tools as needed. The appendixes are the extra drawers in the toolbox with additional information and resources.

Water is the ultimate equalizer: five of these paddlers have a significant disability.
Photo courtesy of K. Schlicher.

Read and use the entire guidebook because each chapter offers a piece of the structure. Also, use this guidebook in conjunction with appropriate general canoeing, kayaking, or coastal kayaking instruction guides listed in the resources in appendix A and on the American Canoe Association Web site under Instruction.

That's it! In this book you have the tools to get started. Follow the guidelines. Use the information that fits the paddler's needs. Above all, work *with* the paddler. Together you can do it. The joy of paddling is waiting and you are the key!

References

National Organization on Disability. (2007). Retrieved August 2, 2008, from www.nod.org.

University of California at San Francisco Disability Statistics Center. *Mobility device use in the United States.* Retrieved August 6, 2008, from http://dsc.ucsf.edu/publication.php?pub_id=2&section_id=4.

U.S. Census Bureau. *U.S. interim projections by age, sex, race, and hispanic origin: 2000-2050.* (2008). Retrieved August 8, 2008, from www.census.gov/population/www/projections/usinterimproj.

General Guidelines

Any journey into new territory is smoother and more productive for everyone when the rules of the road are clear from the beginning. Integrating people who have disabilities into paddling is such a journey. This chapter offers a framework for approaching the concept of disability, tips on appropriate terminology, strategies for interacting with individuals who have disabilities, and perspectives on risk management. These are the basic guidelines—the rules of the road you need to make everyone more comfortable as you work together in your instructional setting or program.

What to Say

The phrases and terms we use create the atmosphere in which we function. Although individuals who have disabilities use a variety of terms to refer to themselves, it is essential that instructors and program providers use terminology that is considered acceptable by the majority of people and that complies with the language used in the 1990 Americans with Disabilities Act as well as other federal laws and regulations.

The two terms most commonly used to describe a person who has a limitation are *handicapped* and *disabled*. A disability is the result of a medically definable condition that limits a person's movements, senses, mental function, or activities. A handicap is a barrier or circumstance that makes progress or success difficult, such as an impassable flight of stairs or a negative attitude toward a person who has a disability.

Here is a practical example: A paddler who has quadriplegia (some level of paralysis in all four limbs) has been told that she doesn't look handicapped when she is paddling her sea kayak. Think about the situation. When she paddles her sea kayak, she glides smoothly through the water. No barriers stop, or handicap, her, but she still has a disability.

The correct term is *disability*—a person with a disability. Person-first terminology is used because the person is more important than the disability. Examples of person-first terminology include the person who is blind instead of the blind person and the person who uses a wheelchair rather than the wheelchair person or the wheelchair-bound person. Although people who have disabilities may have physical or cognitive impairments, they are neither victims nor sufferers; they are people.

A person who has a disability may call himself anything he wishes; however, it is important that instructors and program providers use the most appropriate and acceptable terminology. Keep in mind that the term *handicapped* has a negative connotation when referring to a person who has a disability. The word has existed for

5

The freedom of leaving the wheelchair behind.

centuries, but it was not used to refer to people with disabilities until the late 1800s. Many people believe that the term *handicapped* was first used to refer to Civil War veterans whose injuries prevented them from working and who were therefore begging on the streets with "cap in hand." Because the story has become legend and begging for a living is degrading, describing people with disabilities as handicapped is offensive to many who have disabilities. Therefore, to avoid offending people, avoid the term *handicapped*.

The federal and state governments have recognized this problem and replaced the term *handicapped* with person-first terminology in laws, regulations, and policies as they are developed or reauthorized. The 1990 Americans with Disabilities Act, as well as state and other federal legislation since the early 1990s, use only the term *disability* when referring to people who have a significant limitation of one or more of their major life activities.

Buzzwords such as *differently abled, physically challenged,* and *specially enabled* dance around a disability and only serve to highlight it. There is no need to pretty up the term *disability*; a disability is a fact of life. Rather than trying to minimize it by calling it something else, acknowledge the fact of the disability, discover the individual, adapt for the loss of function caused by the disability, and move the focus to integrating all people in the opportunity. Emphasize ability; what people can do is more important than what they cannot do.

What to Do

We all want to feel comfortable with each other. When you encounter a person who has an obvious disability, you should focus on the person, not the disability. Use the sidebar Tips for Interacting With People With Disabilities on page 7 for additional guidance.

A person who has a disability and is interested in canoeing or kayaking has probably come to grips with the limitations caused by the disability and is relatively independent. Give her room to use her ability. State once that you are willing to give any help; she need only ask. Then leave it at that. What may appear to you to be an awkward struggle may be the person's normal way to function. Do not keep asking, "May I help you?" Once you have made a clear offer to assist, you should assume that the person will ask for your help if needed. Repeated offers only indicate your discomfort with her efforts to be independent.

Always include the person who has a disability in any conversation that involves him. An example is the process of deciding how to transfer from a wheelchair to a waiting canoe or kayak. The person who uses the wheelchair is the expert on how to transfer from the chair to another location. You, as the experienced paddler, know how the canoe or kayak will react when the person's weight encounters the craft and understand the underlying safety issues involved with entering a boat. Talk through the process with the person who uses the wheelchair to determine the

Tips for Interacting With People With Disabilities

- Remember that people are still people despite a wide range of abilities.
- Relax!
- Look directly at the person and maintain eye contact.
- When having a long conversation with a person who is in a wheelchair, stoop down or sit nearby so that you are closer to the same eye level.
- Do not lean on or use a person's wheelchair, crutches, or other mobility devices without permission.
- Ask first if assistance is needed; do not assume that assistance is needed or wanted.
- Speak as you would normally. For example, if speaking to a person who has a mobility impairment, you do not need to avoid words such as *run* and *walk*. If speaking to a person who is blind, you can say, "See you later."
- When speaking to a person who is deaf or hard of hearing, be sure the person has a clear view of your mouth. Keep hands, food, and props away from your mouth while you are speaking. Ideally, mustaches should be cut short so the upper lip can be seen clearly.
- If a sign language interpreter is interpreting your conversation, speak to and look at the person to whom you are speaking—not the interpreter.
- When speaking to a person who has a visual impairment, be sure to introduce yourself by name. Use the clock method to assist the person in locating or avoiding objects or places. The clock method uses the numbers of the clock for reference points: straight in front of the person is 12:00, directly behind is 6:00.
- Don't shout.

safest and most respectful way to complete that transfer. Potential transfer processes are explained in chapter 10, Transfers and Carries.

Risk Management

Safety is the primary consideration for all paddlers whether or not they have a disability. You need to manage the risk in activities at all times and introduce new skills and challenges only as each paddler is ready for them.

The inherent risk in water-based activities is a concern for everyone. However, some people may view individuals with a disability as being less capable or more vulnerable. To a person with that misperception, the element of risk is often exaggerated by the fact of a disability with the result that they may think canoeing or kayaking is too risky an activity for a person who has a disability. For some people with disabilities, risk is the adventurous edge to the sport that gives them a sense of satisfaction and raises their self-esteem.

Risk for all paddlers must be managed at an acceptable level. It is your responsibility to inform each paddler of the involved risks. Paddlers have the right to risk their own safety but not the safety of others, including potential rescuers. Within those constraints, the ultimate decision to participate belongs to the individual, regardless of disability.

The American Canoe Association provides a framework for safely enjoying paddling opportunities in their paddler's safety checklist. The basic principles are summarized here. The complete safety checklist is available at the American Canoe Association Web site (www.americancanoe.org). Type "paddler's safety checklist" in the search field to find it.

1. Know the waters to be paddled. River guide booklets and topographic maps are valuable references in trip planning. Plan alternative routes.

2. Set up locations for put-ins and take-outs along with possible lunch break stops. Consider time and distance. Arrange for the shuttle.

3. What you take with you on a trip is all that you have to survive and rescue yourself. This includes water, food, maps and charts, equipment, and extra clothes.

4. File a float plan with someone who will notify others if you don't return on time.

5. Unless the trip is an instructional or a commercially guided trip, most trips are of a common adventure trip format where each participant takes responsibility for personal participation, the selection of appropriate equipment, and the decision to run or scout rapids. More experienced paddlers should assist those less experienced in making proper decisions on the trip.

6. Paddle within both your and your group's limits.

7. Be a competent swimmer with the ability to handle oneself underwater, in moving water, surf, or current.

8. Have a properly fitted life jacket (personal flotation device [PFD]), and WEAR IT!

9. Keep the craft under control. Do not enter a rapid unless reasonably sure you can navigate it or swim the entire rapid in case you capsize.

10. Be sure to keep an appropriate distance between craft (a good general rule is to keep the craft behind you in view). Normally, stay behind the lead and be in front of the sweep boat. Both the lead and sweep boats should be experienced boaters.

11. Keep a lookout for hazards and avoid them. Watch for fog, especially on coastal waters.

12. Know your emotional and physical limitations. Group members need to constantly assess the behavior of others in their group.

13. Respect the rights of anglers and land owners when paddling.

River paddlers must also be familiar with the International Scale of River Difficulty. This scale can help each paddler understand the American system of rating river types, which combined with local knowledge and other resources can help paddlers select rivers appropriate to their skills. The scale is available on the American Whitewater Web page at www.americanwhitewater.org/content/Wiki/safety:start.

Legal Requirements

Accessibility of Facilities and Programs

To fulfill their legal responsibilities, all instructors and program leaders need to understand the laws addressing disability and accessibility to programs and facilities. This chapter explains how those legal requirements affect your paddling program and provides useful advice for developing accessible programs and facilities.

Basic Legal Requirements

The 1990 Americans with Disabilities Act (ADA) has inspired hope and granted freedom while also causing anxiety and confusion. The good news is that for outdoor programs the ADA lays out clear guidelines for full compliance with the law. This section addresses specific responsibilities and practical steps to follow to ensure that your program remains in full compliance with the law.

Since the passage of Section 504 of the Rehabilitation Act (1973), all federal agencies and those operating under permits issued by federal agencies have been required to ensure that people with disabilities have an equal opportunity to participate in their programs. In 1990 the ADA extended that requirement to all state and local government services, public accommodations (businesses open to the public), and public transportation. Religious organizations and private clubs, which are not open to the public, are the only entities exempt from the requirement to integrate people with disabilities. For the sake of simplicity, this guidebook refers only to the ADA requirements.

If you operate your business in whole or in part under a permit from a federal agency, such as the U.S. Forest Service, Bureau of Land Management, or National Park Service, the accessibility requirements for your structures may be more stringent. Contact your permit administrator for more information.

To understand the ADA, it is important to remember several key points. First, the ADA is essentially civil rights legislation designed to protect the rights of people with disabilities in employment, public transportation, services of state and local governments, and programs and activities offered to the public.

The ADA covers both facility access and access to programs and services. In other words, not only must buildings be accessible, but also the activities that take place within and outside those buildings must be accessible. The law emphasizes independence, integration, and dignity. We will look first at facility access and then at program access.

Facility Access

If people must enter a facility to participate in a program, then access by people with disabilities is required under the ADA. If you own, operate, or lease a business that serves the public, or lease to a business that serves the public, then you must provide access to your facilities as well as to any alterations or new construction. There are no provisions in the law that exempt or grandfather the program inside an existing building from the requirement to be accessible.

New construction and altered facilities must be in compliance with the current accessibility standards. Privately owned businesses are required to use the ADA standards for accessibility (which can be found at www.access-board.gov) or the local or state code, whichever has more stringent requirements for new construction and alterations.

The accessibility guidelines are based on access for a person using a wheelchair. The wheelchair is the determinant of accessibility. If a person using a wheelchair can get into a building and participate in the activities inside that building, then it is likely that other people with disabilities can also access that building. Therefore, it is considered accessible to all people. However, to a more limited degree the guidelines also address access by people who are deaf or hard of hearing and by those who are blind or have limited vision.

Because everyone appreciates more room in a restroom, among other tight places, accessible design is being viewed as good universal design because it works well for everyone. The basic requirement is that whatever is provided to all participants in the program is also provided to the person who has a disability and is qualified for the program.

Evaluating Facilities

We understand that new facilities have to be accessible, but what about existing facilities? Again, the facility must be accessible if a person has to enter it to participate in the program being offered. Following are basic questions to ask to determine whether a facility is accessible:

- Are all doorways a minimum of 32 inches (81 cm) wide?
- Is there 60 inches (152 cm) of clear space inside and outside the doors?
- Do the restroom and changing room have a 60-inch (152 cm) turning radius?
- Does the restroom meet the ADA accessibility standards for grab bars, heights, and reach ranges?
- Do doors have lever handles rather than knobs?
- Do parking lots and walkways have firm and stable surfaces?
- Do parking lots and walkways have a minimum of 36 inches (91 cm) of clear width?

A checklist for easy evaluation of existing facilities is available on the ADA Web page at www.ada.gov/racheck.pdf. This checklist will help you identify accessibility problems and solutions in existing facilities in order to meet your obligations under the ADA to make an existing facility more usable for people with disabilities, while providing access to the program inside the building.

There is a handy rule of thumb when evaluating a surface. The purpose of ensuring the firmness and stability of a surface is to prevent mobility devices (crutches, a cane, or a wheelchair) from sinking into the surface, thereby making it difficult for a person to move through the area with reasonable effort. The primary mobility device used for measurement purposes in the accessibility guidelines is the wheel-chair because its dimensions and multiple moving surface contact points (its four wheels) often make it difficult to accommodate. Thus, if a person using a wheelchair can use an area, most other people can also.

To determine whether a surface is firm and stable enough to accommodate a person using a wheelchair, look at the surface and consider two questions:

1. Could a person riding a narrow-tired bicycle cross the surface easily without the wheels sinking into or disturbing the surface?

2. Could a heavy child in a folding umbrella stroller with small plastic wheels be pushed across that surface without the small wheels sinking into or distorting the surface?

The configurations of bicycle wheels and umbrella stroller wheels are similar to those of the large rear wheels and small front casters of the average wheelchair. See the sidebar Tips for Crossing Beaches or Rough Terrain With a Wheelchair on this page.

If the facility or site is not independently accessible, warn people with disabilities *before* they arrive. In printed or electronic materials for your program, state: "If you have special needs, please call (list a name and number)." People can then determine whether they have a special need about which they need to check with you. Their need may be for a babysitting service, a nearby location where they can get lunch, or wheelchair accessibility.

Tips for Crossing Beaches or Rough Terrain With a Wheelchair

Most beaches do not meet the firm and stable criteria required of an accessible surface. A variety of temporary, portable surface systems have been used over the years for crossing surfaces like this. The most convenient and durable had been heavy-duty rolls of ski race fencing that were easy to stow and carry. Unfortunately, they are no longer available. Reliable Racing, the original source, now sells only a more flexible ski race fencing system that uses a post system to remain upright. However, it is not rigid enough to serve as a wheelchair-accessible beach surface.

Two lengths of rigid-backed carpet runner, at least 36 inches (91 cm) wide, may be useful, depending on the weight of the wheelchair and the person. Keep in mind that a motorized wheelchair often weighs 250 pounds (113 kg) before adding the weight of the person. Two carpet sections can be used leap-frog style as the person moves across the beach.

Technique for crossing rough terrain.
Photo courtesy of S. Fleischman.

Another means of crossing a beach or rough terrain, usable only with a manual wheelchair, requires a team approach. This strategy does not meet the legal criteria for accessibility that is based on facilitating independent access because it requires the assistance of others, but it is a way to move across difficult terrain without being carried. While the person is seated, tip the wheelchair onto its large rear wheels and pull it backward. One assistant at the back of the wheelchair walks backward, while another assistant grasps the front legs to stabilize the chair while pushing and walking forward. Other team members can serve as spotters and help clear the route.

Costs

The ADA states that retrofits and alterations to make a facility accessible must be "readily achievable," which means that they can be achieved without undue difficulty or expense. The ADA's "readily achievable" requirement is based on the size and resources of the business. Larger businesses with more resources are expected to take a more active role in removing barriers than small businesses are. The ADA also recognizes that economic conditions vary. When a business has resources to remove barriers, it is expected to do so; but when profits are down, barrier removal may be reduced or delayed. Barrier removal is an ongoing obligation; businesses are expected to remove barriers as resources become available.

If it would cost too much to alter the facility, you must find another way to ensure that the services (programs) available to other customers are also available to those who can't enter the facility due to inaccessibility. Creativity is often required to think of an alternative, integrated method of providing access. For example, at a very small privately owned campground store with several steps at the entrance, a doorbell could be placed at the base of the stairs. When a person who is unable to climb the stairs rings the bell, the person operating the store can go outside to the customer and complete the transaction. The other options are limited only by the imagination.

Businesses do not have to make every facility or every part of an existing facility accessible to and usable by people with disabilities. However, such people must be able to obtain the services and participate in the program offered in the facility in the same way that people who do not have disabilities can. Options include moving services to accessible buildings or alternative accessible sites, altering facilities to make them accessible, or constructing new accessible facilities.

However, in accordance with the ADA, businesses must offer alternative accessible programs "in the most integrated setting to obtain the full benefits of the program" and do so with dignity. For example, in an existing multistory building that does not have an elevator but has a restaurant on the top floor, a smaller dining area could be established on the first floor that offers the same menu and services as the restaurant on the top floor. *Caution:* The alternative first-floor restaurant cannot be only for people with disabilities because in that case it would not meet the legal requirement for the most integrated setting. The first-floor service must also be available to people who do not have disabilities.

The good news is that tax credits are available for improving accessibility. Information is available at www.irs.gov. Other resources include *The ADA Guide for Small Businesses*, a tax incentives booklet, available at www.ada.gov.

Also, if participants do not have to enter a facility to participate in the program, then no facility access is required. For example, if you offer paddling instruction but meet the students at the launch area and don't use any other facilities, then there are no facility accessibility issues.

Accessibility at Launching and Landing Sites

There are no legal requirements for accessibility at "carry-down craft" (canoe and kayak) launching areas other than the accessible parking space requirements when there are more than four designated parking spaces. However, the ADA does require that programs be accessible.

A launch area should have a firm and stable surface and not too much of an angle. The use of mobility devices (walkers, canes, crutches, wheelchairs) in launching areas can be difficult at docks or where the surface has sand, steep terrain, or is uneven. An excellent launching area for use by someone who uses a mobility device is a boat ramp. Although a boat ramp angle is steeper than the ideal at 13 to 17 percent (to facilitate sliding boats from vehicle trailers), the firm and stable surface connects directly to the parking lot, eases movement with a mobility device across the surface, and aids transfer into the partially floating canoe or kayak at the base of the ramp.

Getting ready to launch.
Photo courtesy of Northeast Passage-NH.

If no good launch site options are available, it may be necessary to carry a person to the canoe or kayak. In this case, you cannot advertise the program as accessible. Keep in mind that there is no dignity in being carried. Always tell people who use mobility devices *before* they come to participate in the program that the area is not accessible and alternative means, such as carries, will need to be used. Accurate expectations are important to all. See the sidebar Tips for Crossing Beaches or Rough Terrain With a Wheelchair on page 11.

Mobility Device Security

The security of a person's wheelchair and other mobility devices is vital. A person who leaves behind a mobility device to go paddling may feel as though she left her legs behind. This person will be concerned. Never leave an empty wheelchair or other mobility device unattended. Lock the device in a building or return it to a vehicle. Discuss such security options with the person who uses the mobility device before she gets into the boat. The person may need to show you how to stow the device in a vehicle or operate a wheelchair lift. Plan ahead because once people are in their canoes or kayaks, such training will be very difficult.

Safety Issues

Do accessibility needs and safety concerns conflict in outdoor programming? No. Many perceived conflicts are based on stereotypes and misinformation about access measures. There is no need to compromise client or staff safety to provide for accessibility. Safety must never be compromised. Medical issues can affect safety; therefore, completion of the medical information sheet (see appendix B) by all parties is essential and is discussed in chapter 4.

Program Access

What is a program? Simply put, a program is the reason a person visits the area. At a campground it is camping and also access to the restroom, water, swimming beach, and other program opportunities offered at that site. At an outfitters' store the program is looking at, trying on, and hopefully purchasing the clothing, equipment, and accessories for sale. It might also be registering for a trip or paddling instruction.

An underlying ADA concept is that each person has the right to participate in programs and activities in an integrated setting with dignity and as much independence as possible, whether or not the person has a disability. This dignified participation occurs only when each person is recognized as an individual with his or her own interests and abilities. Although people with disabilities comprise the largest minority in the country, they are not alike. There is no single disability culture or way of thinking. To truly see the individual, we must put aside stereotypes of people who have disabilities.

The ADA requires that decisions for employment and program participation not be based on stereotypes. Service providers cannot base their decisions simply on the fact that a person carries the label of a disability whether or not that disability is obvious. Instead, participation must be determined by what that person can do. The only question is whether the person can perform the basic functions required of the program or activity according to the eligibility criteria applied to each participant. If the answer is yes, then the person must be allowed to participate in the program or activity under the same rules and requirements as all other participants (ADA Title III Section 302). We discuss essential eligibility criteria development in more depth later in this chapter on page 15.

The ADA requires that programs be modified to accommodate individuals with disabilities unless modifying a program would fundamentally alter that program. For example, transporting an individual with a disability by motorized vehicle in an area closed to motorized use would be a fundamental alteration of that program and should not be allowed.

Reasonable accommodation is an employment term and process. It is the requirement that the employer provide whatever is needed for the employee to be able to fulfill the essential functions of a job (within a reasonable cost). Reasonable accommodation is not part of programmatic (non-employment-based) legal requirements. These program-related, nonemployment aspects of the laws do not require that changes be made to suit each person's needs.

The ADA and federal laws (Section 504, on which the ADA was modeled) require that people with disabilities be able to fulfill the essential criteria for participation in the program. People with disabilities should be able to participate in the same way as everyone else who wishes to participate in that program, but without modifications to the program. For example, if motorized vehicles are not allowed in a specific area, a person would not be allowed to take an ATV into that area simply because of a disability. Use of a motor vehicle would fundamentally alter the program in that nonmotorized area for all people.

Integrated Setting

The accessibility laws state that programs must be provided in the most integrated setting possible. The most integrated setting is the one that enables as much interaction as possible among people with and without disabilities.

People with disabilities who meet the essential eligibility criteria may not be denied the right to participate in any activity, even if a separate program for people with disabilities is available. Separate programs specifically for people with disabilities are acceptable only when necessary to provide equally effective benefits and services.

Programs are not required to guarantee successful participation, but they must offer equal opportunity for participation. For example, no program is required to guarantee that participants will catch a fish of a certain size on a fishing trip, reach the summit of a particular mountain they set out to climb, or even reach a particular location to which they hike. The participant is merely setting out to reach that goal. In the same way, the program is not required to guarantee that each person will achieve exactly what he or she sets out to do just because the person has a disability. The requirement is that the person is to have an equal opportunity to try to reach the goal along with everyone else who meets the criteria for participation in that program.

The laws require that a person not be turned away from a paddling program solely because of a disability. However, that person must complete the medical information sheet, answer the related questions, and be evaluated through the program's essential eligibility criteria, just as all potential participants must complete the same process.

Developing Essential Eligibility Criteria

Essential eligibility criteria takes the guesswork out of who should participate in your program. It gives potential participants and the program providers the information they need to make an accurate and objective assessment when deciding if the participant's abilities are appropriate to participate safely in the activity. Essential eligibility criteria are simply the essential skills each participant is required to perform for safety in that activity, in accordance with the Americans with Disabilities Act (ADA) Title III Section 302 (b) (2) (A) (i) requirement that eligibility criteria be equally applied to all potential participants.

Paddling instructors, outfitters, and paddling program providers provide a wide spectrum of activities and programs. The purpose of essential eligibility criteria is to establish whether a person can participate in an activity based on his ability to perform the activity's basic functions. To participate in an activity, all potential clients must be able to meet the nondiscriminatory essential eligibility criteria established by the instructor, outfitter, or program provider for that specific activity.

The essential eligibility criteria for each program must be provided to all potential clients. It can be posted on a Web site as a portion of the specific program's description, on any materials provided to the potential client, and as part of the registration materials signed by the client. The key is that the essential eligibility criteria must be applied to all potential clients. If the essential eligibility criteria are applied only to potential clients who have disabilities, the criteria would likely be considered discriminatory when challenged legally.

In reality, most instructors, outfitters, and program providers already apply the concept of essential eligibility criteria to potential clients. They use the guidelines in determining which potential clients are likely to be able to participate safely in the program. The problem is that the criteria for many programs are only in the programmer's head rather than in writing. As a result, two mistakes can be made in applying the criteria to a potential participant with a disability:

• *Subjectivity*. The guidelines are often subjective because most instructors, outfitters, and program providers pass on their teaching traditions orally, which invites inconsistency. This approach could spell trouble if they are ever challenged on whether they apply the criteria equally to everyone. You need to document your eligibility criteria carefully.

• *Stereotyping*. Many program providers are forced to make quick assessments of potential clients' abilities without any real knowledge of their capabilities. Many people have stereotypes about the abilities of people with disabilities. When these stereotypes shape the decision-making process, the chances increase of unfairly assessing the ability of a potential client with a disability, resulting in discrimination.

The purpose of developing essential eligibility criteria is to give you and the potential client the information you need to make an accurate, objective assessment when deciding whether the person's abilities are appropriate for the program. You must be able to explain clearly the criteria for participation to the potential participant. It must not be designed or tend to screen out an individual with a disability or any class of individuals with disabilities from an equal opportunity to participate. Instead, the criteria must be based on functional components necessary for remaining safe and be applied equally to every potential client. Instead of disqualifying a person from registering for a course or a trip because the potential client uses a wheelchair, you must use the same eligibility criteria for safe participation as you use with all potential participants.

The model suggested here is similar to that of job descriptions required of employers. Employers must identify the essential and nonessential functions of a job and then determine whether the person can perform those essential functions. Following this logic, you must identify the basic eligibility criteria necessary for people to participate safely in your program or activity. That information should be posted, and each potential participant must be given the opportunity to evaluate his or her ability to meet those criteria. If a person states that she can meet the safety-based participation criteria and then is unable to, she can be removed from the program.

Steps to Developing Nondiscriminatory Essential Eligibility Criteria

Developing guidelines for what your clients must be able to do should be an easy process. You probably already have guidelines in your head; you just need to write them down in a nondiscriminatory way. Think of this step as an exercise in writing down commonsense functions, and you are well on the way to success! The key is that essential eligibility criteria focus on ability rather than disability. Referring to an activity in terms of who can participate, rather than in terms of who can't, counteracts the tendency to stereotype what a person with a disability can do. Follow these steps:

1. Think in terms of the physical and mental abilities necessary for participation in your programs and activities. What does it take to participate in the specific activities of your program such as getting into a canoe or sea kayak and using a paddle? Do participants have to be able to think quickly? Do they have to be strong? Do they have to be able to understand directions? Does your program require an understanding of highly technical factors? Could adaptive equipment be used?

2. Divide the activity into the basic stages of participation (i.e., putting on equipment, using equipment, and returning equipment to a specific area). In effect, you need to separate the program into the discrete activities or variables that make it up. Could a companion safely assist a person in the completion of the task?

3. Consider the abilities necessary for remaining safe. What are the most likely causes of death or injury involved with that activity, and what do participants need to do to avoid them?

4. Prioritize the stages described in step 2 into the critical abilities necessary for safety. For example, when paddling a canoe, the ability to remain seated and balanced (with support if needed) is a higher safety priority than the ability to execute specific paddle strokes.

5. Do not use limiting words such as walk, climb, or see. Instead, describe the result that must be achieved in nondiscriminatory terms, such as access, ascend, or identify.

6. Consider basic rules of etiquette that participants must follow. These issues may include yielding to others who have the right of way or waiting for the rest of the group to catch up.

7. Determine whether the guidelines may be satisfactorily met with the help of a companion. A person may not be able to perform a function independently, but might easily do it with the help of a friend or family member.

8. Edit for simplicity. Stick to the basic physical or mental abilities necessary for participation—the fewer the better.

The following examples are possible essential eligibility requirements for a paddling program.

Example 1
Use of a canoe at a rental facility, on a guided trip, or at a day camp

- *Equipment:* Participants must wear all protective equipment recommended or required by industry standards.
- *Entering and exiting:* Participants must be able to enter and exit the canoe independently or with the assistance of a companion, staff member, or counselor.
- *Seating:* Participants must be able to remain seated and balanced, using adaptive support if necessary.
- *Paddling:* At least one person in the canoe must have the ability to move it through the water in a stable manner and take it to the designated landing area.
- *Safety:* In the event of a capsize, the canoeists must have:
  - *Wet exits:* The ability to get out independently from under the watercraft.
  - *Self-rescue:* The ability to right oneself, remain faceup in the water with the aid of a life jacket, and make progress to the shoreline.
- *Land activities:* Participants must be able to move about the camp independently or with the assistance of a companion on trips, including overnight camping.

Example 2
An ACA flatwater Quick Start (3-hour) or Introduction to Paddling (6-hour) session

- Each participant must be 18 years or older or accompanied by an adult.
- Each participant must be able to manage all personal care and mobility independently or with the assistance of a companion who accompanies them.
- Each participant must be able to get in and out of a kayak independently or with the assistance of a companion following instruction.
- Each participant must be comfortable in the water including floating on his or her back independently with a properly fitted life jacket, turning from facedown to faceup independently while wearing a properly fitted life jacket, and holding his or her breath while under water.
- Each participant must be able to maintain a balanced, upright position when seated in a kayak with adaptations if needed. *Note:* No adaptations providing head or neck support will be accepted.

Providing Nondiscriminatory Essential Eligibility Criteria

You will need to inform your potential clients of your essential eligibility criteria once you have developed them. Because these criteria also serve as an important self-screening tool, potential participants should have an opportunity to read them before they arrive at the program site. Effective ways to share these criteria in advance include posting them on your Web site and in your brochures as well as at your business and where potential participants register for the course, trip, or program.

Accessible Information

About 20 million people are deaf or hard of hearing, so printed information is essential (Deaf/Hard of Hearing Connection, 2005). You also need to be aware of the TTY (text-telephone) Relay System (711).

A TTY is a means of communication used by people who are deaf or hard of hearing, or who have difficulty speaking. The 711 Relay System is a nationwide system established under the ADA. The relay operators have both a TTY, which looks like a small computer keyboard with a narrow LED screen at the top of the keyboard, and a voice phone. People use a TTY to call a relay operator at no charge. The 711 process also allows a business or person who does not have a TTY to call a person who communicates through a TTY. See the sidebar Using the 711 TTY/Relay Call System on this page.

About 10 million people have low vision or are blind (American Federation for the Blind, 2008). Of that number, only a very small percentage are completely blind. Large-print and high-contrast materials are key to reaching the majority of people with limited vision. Given the aging U.S. population, large-print and high-contrast materials will be increasingly important for getting your message to potential customers.

Using the 711 TTY/Relay Call System

When a person who uses a TTY dials 711, the 711 Relay system operator uses the voice phone to place the call. The operator sends the call to the desired business or person who does not have a TTY. The relay operator then acts as an interpreter between the two types of communication devices.

The relay operator tells the person who answers the voice phone that he is receiving a relay call from a specific person calling from a TTY. The person answering the voice phone then says "hello," followed by the name of the person who has placed the call (i.e., "Hello, Mr. Jones"). It is very important to remember that the communication is between the two callers; the relay operator is an invisible communication link and should not be addressed during the call. For example, one should not say to the operator: "Tell Mr. Jones I say hello."

After the person answering the voice phone has greeted the caller, the relay operator types that greeting message into the operator's TTY for the person placing the TTY call to read. That person replies via TTY, and the relay operator reads the TTY message over the voice phone to the other person. This process continues until the conversation is finished. At that time one of the parties says "SK" (stop-keying), which is equivalent to good-bye, to indicate no further conversation. If the other party has nothing further to add, the person says "good-bye" and then "SK," indicating the end of the conversation.

References

American Federation for the Blind. (2008). *Living with vision loss.* Retrieved April 20, 2009, from www.afb.org/Section.asp?SectionID=40.

Deaf/Hard of Hearing Connection. (2005). *Facts about hearing loss.* Retrieved August 8, 2008, from www.dhhc.org/facts.html.

Instructor Checklists

Effective paddling instruction requires specific information and planning. This chapter provides the tools you need to get ready, including a number of checklists to use to gather medical information, interview the paddler, and talk through disability-related issues. We also address selecting locations for instruction and open-water paddling trips, safety considerations, and emergency response preparation. Reading, planning, and using the tools provided here will help you offer a successful instructional experience to all participants.

Program Overview

The safety, enjoyment, and skill development of each participant are the goals of paddling instruction. The ACA instructional courses provide the teaching sequences that introduce new skills, risks, and challenges as paddlers are ready for them. With safety and enjoyment as priorities, the instructor follows a sequence from preprogram preparation to dry-land orientation, calm-water practice, and a calm-water trip. Additional practice sites with a variety of environmental conditions further develop the paddlers' skills as they work through wind, waves, and current in flatwater, whitewater, or the ocean. Depending on students' abilities and learning styles, different teaching techniques and more time may be needed to achieve these goals.

These basic program elements apply for all paddling students, whether or not they have disabilities. Once the appropriate adaptation is in place that compensates for a person's loss of function as a result of a disability, then the remainder of instruction follows the same sequence for all students.

This book is not a detailed guide to all aspects of paddling or paddling instruction; it supplements the technical information found in the ACA-endorsed manuals. Nevertheless, you are reading this book because you want to appropriately integrate paddlers who have a disability into the sport. To that end, make use of the tools this book gives you and incorporate the information into your planning. Have all students fill out the medical information sheet (MIS) in appendix B, and complete a detailed paddler's interview with each person (see appendix C). Use chapter 6, Disabilities and Their Implications for Paddling and Instruction, to learn about specific disabilities, and let the teaching suggestions guide you in developing a positive experience for your participants. Lastly, use chapters 7 and 8 to develop any needed equipment adaptations.

The topics in each of the following checklists have proven to be vital components of any integrated paddling instruction. A discussion of each topic follows in the related sections of this guide.

Preprogram Preparation Checklist

❑ Medical information sheet

❑ Paddler's interview

❑ Group or private instruction

❑ Program location: safety and accessibility

❑ Pool vs. outdoor site

❑ Preprogram scouting

❑ Hygiene considerations

❑ Group gear check

❑ Emergency response plan preparation (local emergency phone numbers for police, EMS, evacuation points, agency contact, emergency contacts for participants, group or participant emergency skill sets and certifications)

During-Program Checklist

❑ Equipping paddlers

❑ Adapting the boat

❑ Orientation to entering and launching

❑ Orientation to wet exit and rescue

❑ Entering and launching practice

❑ On-water practice of wet exit and rescue

❑ Orientation to strokes and maneuvers

❑ On-water practice of strokes and maneuvers

❑ Group organization for travel

❑ Advice for participation beyond the program

Postprogram Checklist

❑ Participant feedback

❑ Instructor and volunteer evaluation

❑ Staff debrief of program including the site, equipment, group, and instruction

❑ What worked?

❑ What could be better?

❑ How will we do it differently next time?

From J. Zeller, 2009, *Canoeing and Kayaking for People With Disabilities* (Champaign, IL: Human Kinetics).

Medical Information Sheet

The medical information sheet (MIS) is a comprehensive, nondiscriminatory summary of medical information related to paddling to be completed by every person before participation (see appendix B). Its purpose is to give you the information necessary to be aware of any potential problems and to help participants safely enjoy canoeing or kayaking. Completed medical information sheets tell you who is allergic to bee stings, has diabetes or a heart problem, or is greatly affected by heat or cold, among other issues.

Confidentiality of Medical Information

A person's medical information is confidential under the law and is *not* to be discussed with others without that person's permission. Disclosure (explanation to others) must be discussed with the person if the person's disability is not obvious but is likely to affect others in the class or activity group. Never disclose any medical information without the person's approval. If a person participating in your program has a disability that is not obvious but has the potential to affect others in the group, discuss with that person the need to disclose the aspects of the disability that may affect others. If the person is willing to disclose the disability, thereby revealing some of the medical information, it should be done at the first group meeting. If the person prefers that you explain to the group, work with the person to determine what you will say. For example, if the person has some loss of hearing, the statement to the group may be as simple as: "Sue has difficulty hearing, but she does read lips. So please be sure Sue is looking at you when you speak to her."

If the person is unwilling to permit disclosure, you must decide whether the person can participate without putting the safety of others in jeopardy. Disclosure can become a primary concern during the program if not addressed before it begins.

Disclosure Case Study

Scene: On an extended wilderness trip, one of the participants had a disability that was not obvious but caused fatigue, which was at times debilitating. He adamantly refused to allow the trip leaders to disclose his disability to the other participants. During the trip he paddled less than the others and did little of the camp work. The other participants perceived him as lazy and the trip leaders as showing favoritism. The other participants complained to the trip leaders, who again asked the participant to allow disclosure. However, he continued to refuse. The leaders, bound by medical confidentiality, could not discuss the participant's disability with the group.

Issues: As a result of the person's refusal to disclose his disability, there was a potential safety issue because other group members did not understand that he could be incapacitated by his fatigue regardless of the situation the group was in at the time. In addition, group cohesion never developed, which had a negative impact on everyone on the trip.

Solutions: The trip leader or instructor must take the time prior to the program to fully explain to the potential participant that sharing specific disability-related information is important to the health and safety of all. If trip leaders or instructors believe that lack of disclosure would put others in jeopardy, then they may deny participation by that person in that group session. The trip leader or instructor should explain the safety basis for this decision to the potential participant as well as discuss other appropriate venues, such as private instruction, in which disclosure to those other than the instructor would not be necessary.

See the Disclosure Case Study sidebar on page 23 to understand the real implications for your program. If you believe that lack of disclosure would put others in jeopardy, then it would not be safe to allow that person to participate in the program.

Content of the Medical Information Sheet

The recommended MIS form in appendix B asks about specific conditions such as heart disease, back problems, dislocations, and medications. If a person has a specific condition, it does not mean she can't participate in the class or group, only that awareness is important and that precautions or ancillary preparations might need to be made. For example, if a medication makes a person thirsty, then she will need to pack extra water.

Most medications have potential side effects, but the concern during paddling instruction is about side effects that may be exacerbated by exercise, exposure to the sun or cold, or other paddling-related conditions. The MIS asks for yes or no responses regarding medication; it does not ask for a list of all medications. For the sake of medical confidentiality, it is important to ask only for the information essential for the specific activity the questionnaire addresses. People are responsible for knowing the side effects of the medications they are taking and sharing any pertinent side effects with program providers.

The MIS form asks if the person has a disability and later if the person has a mobility or sensory impairment. Those separate questions are not redundant. For example, a person may have a mobility impairment but not view that lack of function as a disability because he has learned to function fully in spite of that disability.

When referring to a spinal cord injury or the impact of a disease affecting the spinal cord, a letter/number combination is often used to specify the location of impact to the spine (e.g., T-12). The letter refers to one of four areas of the spine, and the number refers to the specific vertebra within that area. See Appendix E on page 133 to view the entire spine.

Two people diagnosed at the same level of injury may have very different abilities. The level of injury does not, by itself, define the student's potential. One may be a complete injury and another may be incomplete. In addition, every disability affects the person differently—physically and emotionally. A student's determination also affects potential performance. When uncertain about a student's ability to perform a certain technique, have him try it in a safe environment. See Appendix E for a description of spinal column injuries and related functional losses.

What If a Person Has Had a Seizure?

If a person checks off *seizures* in the MIS, you will need to have a confidential discussion to make additional decisions. Some seizures are infrequent or somewhat predictable, lowering the overall risk. Others may occur frequently or may be less predictable and thus present a much higher level of risk. You will need to determine with the person whether she is a candidate for paddling at that time and in that setting without putting others in jeopardy should a seizure occur and an immediate rescue be needed.

General guidelines have been developed to assist in the decision-making process regarding seizures. See the sidebar Paddling Guidelines for Individuals With Seizures on page 25. Although the goal is to get people on the water with everyone's safety in mind, this issue and related decisions are an essential part of risk assessment and management.

Paddling Guidelines for Individuals With Seizures

Controlled seizures: Seizure free for at least one year. No additional precautions. *Note:* In the state of Michigan, you can receive a driver's license if you have been seizure free for at least one year, so Bay Cliff Health Camp chose that same guideline for giving a "driver's license" to kayak without additional precautions.

Uncontrolled or partially controlled seizures: If seizures have occurred during the past year:

- Carefully interview the person to determine how frequently their seizures occur, if an aura occurs prior to thereby providing some forewarning for the individual, what that may be, and what has happened during their previous seizure(s).
- The person who has a seizure must be a part of the planning for the response if a seizure occurs, but the lead instructor makes the final call based on a risk analysis of individual and group safety.
- The person who has a seizure disorder must wear a type I PFD.
- The person who has a seizure disorder must be in a tandem kayak.
- The tandem kayak must have a shadow boat in position to raft up at any time.
- The kayakers in the tandem and in the shadow boat must have whistles and know a prearranged emergency signal.

In the event of a seizure, the tandem boat immediately rafts up with the shadow boat. An emergency signal is given to alert the lead instructor, and the rest of the group follows directions for an emergency situation.

Paddler's Interview

The paddler's interview is a private discussion with every student with or without a disability before instruction begins. The purpose is to develop a mutual understanding of expectations, estimate the student's ability level, and discuss any concerns.

With a student who has a disability, the discussion will also include implications for paddling as a result of the disability and initial thoughts about possible adaptations. Adaptations compensate for loss of function. However, keep the focus on ability—both physical and mental, that is both the person's physical ability and their willpower. Although each person is affected differently by a disability, the person is the expert on his disability and you are the expert at teaching paddling. Working together, you can find solutions. It is helpful to explain this cooperative approach early in the interview. The use of MIS information and a thoughtful paddler's interview are keys to instructing students who have disabilities. See the complete guidelines for a paddler's interview in appendix C on page 129.

Paddler's interview.
Photo courtesy of Northeast Passage-NH.

The student must have confidence in you as the instructor. This confidence comes from a combination of respect for your ability and experience and a belief that you will listen to the student's concerns. You don't need to know all the answers. You do need to be willing to learn from your student. Open and comfortable communication with the student is essential.

Ask every student these key questions:

- What are your expectations?
- What type of paddling are you interested in—exercise, recreation, competition?
- Does your ability match that type of paddling?
- Are you aware of other paddling options such as sea kayaking, river kayaking, or lake paddling?
- What are your concerns?

With the student's completed medical information sheet in hand, do the following:

- Explain that the information on the MIS and gathered from the paddler's interview is confidential. The purpose is ensuring that you (the instructor) are prepared to help the student have a successful paddling experience.
- Ask if the student has any additional information to add to the form.
- Check whether there is any information that should be discussed.

Students need to understand that they are responsible for informing you about the extent of their abilities and skills. A comfortable conversation with the student will lead to more information exchange. During the paddler's interview, be sure to do much more listening than talking.

With the student who has a disability, if appropriate to the disability, do the following:

- Admit it if you do not know about the disabling condition listed on the MIS. A statement such as, "I'm not familiar with reflex dystrophy" (or whatever the unfamiliar disability-related term might be) will open the subject, and the person with the disability usually takes it from there providing information about that condition which is pertinent to them. While a Web search will provide you with extensive information about various medical terms and conditions, all of that information may not be applicable to the individual who completed the MIS. Because each person is affected differently by their disability, the best resource as to how an individual is affected by a specific condition is that person.
- Ask how long the student has had the disability. Such information may help in understanding the student's emotional response during instruction. Students whose disabilities are more recent may experience frustration in new learning situations. Students who have been sheltered by family and friends may have unrealistic expectations. However, students whose disabilities are longer term are often more prepared to deal with difficulties during instruction. If you have doubts about the experience or ability the student claims to have, you will need to observe the student in an appropriate boat before placement in a class that will require a specific skill level.
- Ask questions about the disability or the management of symptoms that are pertinent to paddling. The student's responses will highlight possible adaptation needs.

Following are a number of things you can do or ask based on the student's disability:

- If the student has some loss of hand function, check on her ability to grasp the paddle by handing her a paddle.

- If the student has some loss of lower-limb function, check on sitting stability. Ask: "If you were seated on the edge of a bed and not holding on and someone pushed you firmly on your shoulder from the side, what would happen?"

- If the student has a visual impairment but has some sight, ask: "What can you see?"

- If the student has very limited vision or is blind, ask: "How do you generally learn how to do new things?" Similar methods might be applicable to paddling instruction.

Here are some other things you could ask that could be useful:

- Ask whether the student anticipates any specific needs. This is an important question to ask especially of students who may not have shared much information during the conversation to this point. By asking the question about special needs this far into the conversation, the student may share additional concerns that he did not feel comfortable sharing either on the MIS or earlier in the discussion.

- Discuss group and private instruction as needed. First, students must meet the essential eligibility criteria for the class or group activity in which they want to participate, once the equipment is adapted. Keep in mind that ability is a sum of determination, willingness to work, and physical function, plus adaptive equipment if needed. Group instruction is appropriate if his ability level will allow the person to progress at an average or above average rate. Private instruction is appropriate if the ability level will *not* allow the person to progress at an average or above average rate or if he prefers private instruction.

- Explain that you will use as much standard equipment as possible and will adapt equipment only as needed. Adaptations should blend into the look of the boat and not look weird. Ask the student to give you feedback on which adaptations or modifications are helpful and which are not. Asking the student to give you feedback on the adaptations during development reinforces the fact that you are a team, that you want and expect the student's participation, and that you will listen. Creative problem solving is a team (instructor/student) responsibility.

In closing the paddler's interview, leave an opportunity for a comfortable discussion of any future disability-related questions. An appropriate ending question might be: "I think those are all the questions I have for now, but I may think of other questions later. If I do, may I ask you then?"

Location

Indoor pools and outdoor sites offer various advantages and disadvantages for integrated paddling instruction. An indoor pool is a great location to begin paddling instruction because the weather and water conditions are always ideal. During early

Pool session.

Photo courtesy of R. Mravetz.

rescue practice the clear water and controlled depth allow you to provide assistance and support as needed while students learn rescue techniques. However, the size of the pool will limit the number of boats and therefore the number of students in the class. Also, the boats must be cleaned inside and out before they are placed in the pool to prevent water contamination.

After the initial pool instruction, paddling in an outdoor setting protected from the force of wind or waves allows novice paddlers to add to their skills and gain confidence. Good choices for the first open-water paddling experience with new paddlers are short tours on lakes with irregular shorelines or in protected harbors that avoid the effect of wind sweeping across the entire lake. The most accessible launching sites have surfaces firm and stable surfaces and intersect with the water at water level. Avoid docks as well as sandy, steep, or uneven surfaces when possible if a paddler uses a mobility device (wheelchair, walker, crutches, or cane).

A caution for tidal areas: Know the effect of tide levels on the launching and landing sites you will be using. Land across a muddy tidal flat will be difficult, especially for paddlers who use mobility aids.

Having the group paddle for a short time and then take a break is a good plan. After the break those who want to continue to paddle can do so. Depending on the boat type and the paddlers' abilities, additional instruction in wind, waves, weather, and moving water issues can be added.

At the conclusion of paddling, share information about appropriate next steps and local paddling opportunities based on the skills the paddlers have demonstrated. From there each participant can decide what type of paddling to pursue and how aggressively to do so.

Preprogram Scouting

Visit the indoor pool you will be using for your program to check the accessibility of the facilities, including parking, the building entrance, access routes throughout the building, changing rooms, showers, and restroom facilities. By using accessible facilities that you have checked in advance, you won't have to change facilities when a person who has a disability registers for a class.

As discussed in Accessibility at Launching and Landing Sites on page 12 in chapter 3, an accessible outdoor site needs a firm and stable surface without too much of an angle. Beyond boat ramps, the angles of which are significant but at least the service is generally firm and stable, it will likely take some scouting to find accessible launch sites. If a toilet facility is provided, it must be accessible. If no toilet facilities are provided for anyone at the site, ensure that all participants know this before they arrive. If you are renting a portable toilet structure, be sure to obtain an accessible model, which is larger and therefore more convenient for all participants.

GROUP GEAR CHECKLIST

It is handy to have a group gear checklist to avoid forgetting necessary and useful items. Following is a standard list, but you should customize your gear list to the needs of those participating in your program. Group gear can include, but may not be limited to, the following:

❏ Life jackets/personal flotation devices (PFDs)

❏ Paddles

❏ Extra paddles

❏ Paddle floats (self-rescue)

❏ Tow rescue bags or belts (group-assisted rescue)

❏ Webbing sling (to aid in reentering kayaks)

❏ First aid kit

❏ Communication system (cell phone, VHF radio, or satellite phone)

❏ Signal system (strobe light or signal mirror)

❏ Repair kit

❏ Maps or charts and map cases

❏ Foghorns

❏ Compasses

The more adventurous the program, the greater the need for safety gear. Adjust your group gear for environmental conditions as well.

From J. Zeller, 2009, *Canoeing and Kayaking for People With Disabilities* (Champaign, IL: Human Kinetics).

EMERGENCY RESPONSE PLAN PREPARATION CHECKLIST

It is important to know the local area and which jurisdictions serve the emergency needs in that region. Once you know that, gather the following information:

- ❑ Local emergency phone numbers for:
  - ❑ EMS
  - ❑ Police
  - ❑ Agency contact
- ❑ Medical forms and emergency contacts for all participants
- ❑ Driving directions to the nearest hospital
- ❑ Evacuation points

In addition, you should make sure to identify to the group the emergency skill sets and certifications of all participants. Also, all participants should know where the emergency information, first aid kits, and emergency equipment are located.

From J. Zeller, 2009, *Canoeing and Kayaking for People With Disabilities* (Champaign, IL: Human Kinetics).

Equipping the Paddler

Participants will enjoy paddling if they are equipped properly for the activity. Every paddler needs to prepare for the possibility of getting wet, whether it's from paddle and wind splash or from an unexpected capsizing. Weather and water conditions greatly affect the way paddlers prepare for the activity.

Selecting Clothing

Two essential characteristics for paddling clothing are protection and comfort. The clothing needs to repel wind and water and to insulate for appropriate body heat retention. Because many disabilities impair circulation, the effects of cold and heat are an increased concern. The greater the chance of immersion and the more severe the paddling conditions, the more protection is needed. Participants should wear proper clothing to prevent hypothermia (a lowering of the body's core temperature that eventually can cause unconsciousness and death) and hyperthermia (a rise of the body's core temperature to unsafe levels).

It is important to recognize the stages of hypothermia. Watch for early signs such as shivering, lack of muscle coordination, skin numbness, mild confusion, mumbling, and irritability. In paddlers with reduced or absent sensation in the extremities, skin numbness or shivering may be absent. Hypothermia occurs most rapidly in a cold, wet, windy environment. Water temperature, reduced physical activity, clothing, body build, and gender are all factors influencing survival in cold water. Consult general outdoor texts or emergency manuals for more detailed information on hypothermia if you are not familiar with the signs, symptoms, and treatment. The ACA and U.S. Coast Guard have published a brochure, "Cold Water Survival," that should be distributed to all participants. It is available for downloading at www.americancanoe.org under Safety. This brochure is part of the ACA's Paddle Smart, Paddle Safe series.

Impaired circulation may also decrease the body's ability to cool itself in hot weather, which can create hyperthermia. Adequate fluid intake on hot days is very important in addition to appropriate clothing layers. Hot weather and exercise may be a trigger for some people who have cognitive impairments and for those who have seizures, which is another reason, during the paddler's interview, to discuss what triggers the person's seizures and the symptoms to watch for. A person who has a complete spinal cord injury will neither shiver nor sweat below the level of that injury, therefore impairing their body's ability to cool or warm it through those involuntary processes. For more information on difficult regulating body temperature, see page 52 in chapter 6, Disabilities and Their Implications for Paddling and Instruction.

Recommended is a versatile layering system that includes underwear, insulation, and a shell (see figure 5.1). Layering of clothing allows paddlers to keep their body temperature at a comfortable level by adding or removing layers as exercise intensity or air temperature changes.

Garments are available in many fabrics. Synthetic fabrics dry quickly and so will be more comfortable and keep participants warmer in the paddling environment. Unless both the air and water temperatures are warm, participants should avoid cotton clothing because it does not dry quickly and is cold and heavy when wet. Wool is the best natural fiber for providing warmth, although it is difficult to dry and can be irritating to sensitive skin.

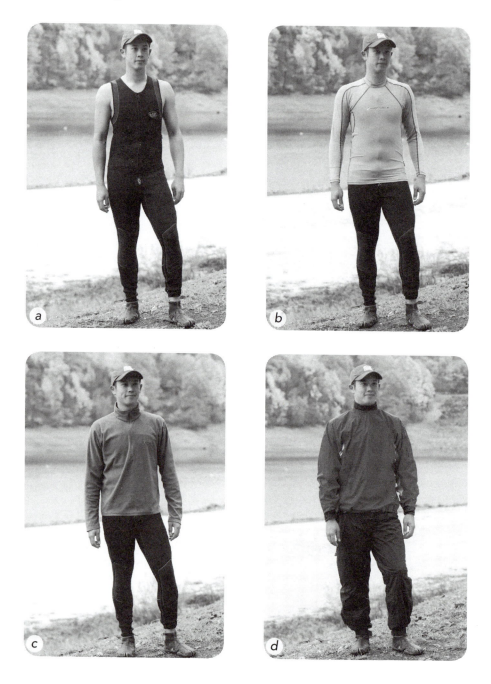

Figure 5.1
Layering.

Waterproof, breathable fabrics (e.g., Goretex, Entrant-DT, Sympatex) keep out the rain while allowing perspiration to escape. If the fabric is waterproof but not breathable (such as coated nylon), perspiration will stay within the garment. The other layers of clothing and the paddler's skin stay wet inside the dry outer shell, resulting in an uncomfortable clammy feeling that can lower body temperature.

The underwear and insulation layers should be made from synthetic fabrics. A nylon bathing suit worn as the underwear layer also facilitates changing clothing in public. Synthetic long underwear keeps people warm even when wet, and the fabric stretches to accommodate splints on the paddler's hands or feet and urinary leg bags.

For the outer layer, paddlers can choose from a wide range of clothing styles to maximize independence. A good choice is loose, comfortable styles that do not bind when sitting in a boat, are easy to put on, and allow a full range of motion. A zip-front paddling jacket may be easier for a person to wear than a pullover or partial zip-front anorak-style jacket, if the paddler has limited range of motion in the shoulder area. Pants with wider legs are much easier to pull on for people who have some loss of leg function, and they also allow for unrestricted use of catheters and leg bags. Dry tops and splash tops that fit snugly over the wrist of a prosthesis trap the prosthesis to the wearer; instead, the person can use short-sleeved dry tops and splash guards or adapt the sleeve and wrist closure of a long-sleeved top.

Wet Suits

When in the water, a barrier (wet suit or dry suit) is the only way to retain heat, although it is not a guarantee against heat loss. A wet suit is made of a thin neoprene layer and allows a paddler to warm a thin water layer between the skin and the wet suit itself (see figure 5.1a). After a capsizing, the wet suit acts as an insulation barrier between the person's body and the colder water on the outside of the wet suit.

Although difficult to get into because they fit the body so closely, wet suits do have several benefits. They provide excellent padding and abrasion resistance for paddlers without sensitivity in their lower limbs. Very important, they also increase the buoyancy of paddlers' legs in the event of a swim. Some wet suits have longer zippers down the chests and up the back of the calves for ease of access. It is also possible to add zippers to a wet suit.

Many instructors favor wet suit vests for some students with lower-limb paralysis because the vests offer good torso insulation and are easier to put on than full-body wet suits. A wet suit vest allows for unrestricted use of a catheter and leg bag. For the lower body, comfortable layers of synthetic long underwear with loose-fitting paddling pants of waterproof nylon are a good combination.

Dry Suits

A dry suit is made of a flexible fabric that does not allow water to pass through it (see figure 5.1d). The dry suit has tight cuffs at the neck, wrists, and ankles to prevent water infiltration. People usually wear insulating underwear underneath dry suits.

Dry suits are better at protecting sensitive skin from constant contact with water than wet suits are. They keep all insulating layers worn underneath them almost completely dry. The looser-fit dry suits are easier to put on, especially for paddlers with lower-limb disabilities, and they allow for unrestricted use of catheters and leg bags. However, dry suits are more expensive than wet suits.

Keeping the head covered is a high priority because so much heat is lost through the head. Wool, polypropylene hats, and wet suit hoods are recommended in cold weather. In warm weather, wetting the head and neck can help keep a person cool. Paddlers can wear wet hats or bandannas.

Before going out on the water, check the weather, including the wind chill factor and water temperature. Some paddlers use a general formula that if the air temperature and the water temperature combined are less than 100 °F (38 °C), wet suits or dry suits should be worn. However, this formula is misleading. For instance, the air temperature could be 80 °F (27 °C), and the water temperature could be 54 °F (12 °C). Using the formula, this combination of temperatures would suggest that paddlers do not need wet suits. However, if paddlers were immersed in 54 °F (12 °C) water, the air temperature would not keep them warm. This formula would apply only if wet paddlers exited the water quickly and the air temperature warmed them up. It does not apply when a paddler may be immersed in cold water for more than 20 minutes. Paddlers must always be prepared because the weather can change quickly. Everyone should bring along a change of clothes in a waterproof bag.

Life Jackets or Personal Flotation Devices (PFDs)

Every paddler should wear a U.S. Coast Guard–approved personal flotation device (PFD) for adequate flotation, physical protection, and warmth. Simply carrying the PFD in the boat does not protect the paddler. PFDs are also commonly called life jackets. A capsize of the boat can occur when you least expect it. The American Canoe Association (2005) states that nearly 70 percent of drownings that involve canoes, kayaks, and rafts might have been prevented if the person had been wearing a life jacket. The best way to prevent a fatality when someone tips unexpectedly is to ensure that everyone wears a life jacket.

In choosing a life jacket, the wearer must consider proper fit and intended use. PFDs are sized according to weight, so wearers should check the label inside it. The life jacket should fit snugly but not too tightly. A loose, oversized vest tends to ride up on the person, interfere with swimming, and force the person's face into the water. Vests that are too small restrict movement and can cause skin abrasion. Side adjustment tabs at the waistband and torso are helpful to allow for various layers of clothing. PFDs should be tried in the water at least once a season because they lose buoyancy over time.

Different styles of PFDs provide different functions. Being familiar with each style will help wearers select the best one for their intended use and as well as their paddling ability. The five styles and their uses are as follows:

Figure 5.2
A type I vest.

• **Type I.** This style provides the most flotation in addition to high buoyancy, warmth, and body protection (see figure 5.2). People who are prone to seizures or have difficulty turning from facedown to faceup in the water should choose this style. However, they should keep in mind that this style of PFD will *not* turn a person who is floating facedown over without some effort on the person's part. This style is bulky and available in a limited range of weight sizes.

• **Type II.** This "horse collar" style is bulky and tends to ride up around the ears in an irritating manner while paddling (see figure 5.3). All ties must be securely fastened, or it may slip off the paddler when the boat capsizes. It does not provide adequate body protection or warmth, and is not recommended for people who will be paddling for an extended time.

Figure 5.3
A type II vest.

• **Type III.** Paddlers use this style most commonly because it is a comfortable vest for continuous, extended wear. Type III vests provide high buoyancy, warmth, support, and body protection from obstacles (see figure 5.4). The vests are available in a variety of styles and size ranges. Short styles are recommended for kayakers and those who have shorter torsos or statures.

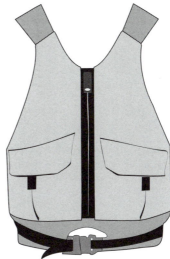

Figure 5.4
A type III vest.

• **Type IV.** This type is a combination boat cushion and throwable device (see figure 5.5), and is not suitable for use as a paddler's PFD.

Figure 5.5
A type IV PFD.

• **Type V.** Special-use devices such as vests, deck suits, and hybrid PFDs are designed for specific activities such as windsurfing, kayaking, or water-skiing (see figure 5.6). Some type V PFDs inflate when you enter the water, and to be acceptable, they must be used in accordance with their labels. Paddlers do not commonly use them.

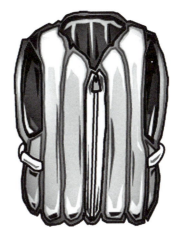

Figure 5.6
A type V vest.

Selecting Canoes and Kayaks

Selecting the most appropriate boat for the paddler requires careful consideration of the person's needs. A kayak designed for a 150- to 175-pound (68 to 79 kg) paddler is not the appropriate boat for the 6-foot, 4-inch, 220-pound (193 cm, 100 kg) man who wants to learn! You undermine satisfaction and safety if the equipment is simply not right for the paddler.

Boat stability is important for most novice paddlers. Your choice of a boat can make an adaptation easier because some designs are inherently more stable than others. The seat may also need to be lowered to enhance stability. If the seating area will be adapted to compensate for the paddler's loss of lower-limb function, the size of the area available in which to make the adaptations is also important. You need enough room to add materials for stability and skin protection.

One consideration is whether to use a solo (one-seat) or tandem (two-seat) boat. This decision should be based on the paddler's ability to control the craft and maintain the proper paddling posture throughout the experience. If a significant mobility impairment limits the lateral stability needed for safe solo paddling, then the person should begin in the bow seat of a tandem craft. This is a logical and safe entry point to the sport and does not preclude the person from paddling in another position at a later point. There should be no stigma to paddling in a tandem craft; it is a great, social way to enjoy a local lake or river and is commonly used on expedition-style trips that require a lot of gear.

Tandem boats are good choices for paddlers who tire quickly and have a significant loss of vision as well as for beginning paddlers who are unable to manage a solo boat. The tandem boat allows the paddler to focus on acquiring basic paddling skills and to build the confidence needed to try a solo boat later if desired. A solo boat works well for most other paddlers, allowing them to set their own pace and direction.

Paddlers should try various styles of canoes and kayaks before buying one. They can decide through instructional or rental programs which canoe or kayak best meets their abilities and intended use. Boat weight and durability are important considerations. If a paddler lacks upper-body strength, a lighter boat may be preferable. A durable boat is the best choice if it will be dragged at the launch or landing site.

Canoes

A canoe generally varies in length from 13 to 18 feet (4 to 5.5 m) and is commonly used on flat- and slow- to moderately moving water (see figures 5.7 and 5.8). Canoes with higher sides have a tendency to catch the wind. Because a canoe is more open

Figure 5.7
An open, solo canoe.

Photos courtesy of Mad
River Canoe.

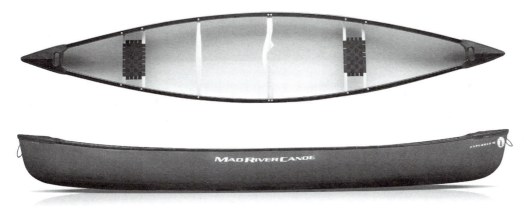

Figure 5.8
A tandem canoe.

Photos courtesy of Mad River Canoe.

than a kayak, it offers easier entry, exit, and access to gear. However, seating stability can be more difficult to adapt in an open canoe because of the large amount of open space.

Adaptation materials often raise the seating position, so it may be (and usually is) necessary to lower the canoe seat for paddlers with disabilities. You can remove the bolts and seat hangers (spacers between the seat and gunwale) and replace them with longer bolts and new seat hangers. The new seat hangers can be made easily from 3/4-inch-diameter (2 cm) PVC pipe. Because the seat is actually hanging from the gunwales, you should provide more support under the seat with Ethafoam. See chapter 7, Adaptation Principles, for more information on types of foam used for seat adaptations.

Three types of canoes are useful for adaptations: recreational canoes, touring canoes, and whitewater canoes.

Recreational Canoes

A recreational canoe is a shorter, wider canoe with good stability that is designed for a variety of purposes from fishing to mild whitewater. Its durability and versatility make it lower in performance than specialized craft. These canoes can range in length from 13 to 16 feet (4 to 5 m). A shorter boat makes turning easier, but traveling in a straight line can be more challenging.

• *Advantages:* They are usually very stable; however, the seat may need to be lowered if a seating adaptation needs to be added. A flat-bottomed hull shape is best. There is adequate room for storing mobility devices, but they should be lashed to the canoe.

• *Disadvantages:* Seat types can vary greatly. Flat, bench-style seats are easier to adapt. In any canoe, if a paddler needs lateral support, you'll need extra time to adapt the seat, including the addition of stable sides to a wider seating area.

Touring Canoes

A touring canoe is longer (about 17 to 18 feet, or 5.2 to 5.5 m, in a tandem) and tracks well in a straight line, but it does not turn easily. Many are designed with good width, flatter bottoms, and adequate volume to carry gear on overnight trips. Low-sided canoes minimize wind resistance but can take on water from waves, so they are best on flatwater. A higher-sided touring canoe is necessary for mild whitewater.

- *Advantages:* These canoes are easier to steer for a person with an upper-limb loss of function. They have very good volume for mobility devices. The bow and stern can be narrower than the bow and stern of a recreational canoe, so seat adaptations can be easier to build on the narrower seat.
- *Disadvantages:* Some boats can be tippier if they have tumblehome (an inward curving of the hull near the gunwales); choose a boat with good initial and secondary stability. A lower-sided boat can increase spray from waves, which can contribute to wet clothing and skin breakdown.

The seat may need to be lowered to maintain trim (balance) if a seating adaptation raises the paddler's balance point. Again, if a paddler needs lateral support, you'll need extra time to adapt the seat and add stable sides to the seating area.

Whitewater Canoes

These shorter boats have more rocker, which is a more curved hull shape from bow to stern, so they can turn more easily in whitewater. They may have less initial stability, which allows them to be leaned to the side for whitewater maneuvers.

- *Advantages:* Tandem canoes allow a novice paddler with a disability to be paired with a skilled canoeist, so both can enjoy the exhilaration of whitewater.
- *Disadvantages:* Seats vary from bench (sitting) to pedestal (kneeling) styles; pedestals can be uncomfortable for paddlers with lower-limb impairments.

Kayaks

Kayaks generally vary in length from 9 to 18 feet (3 to 5.5 m). Longer kayaks tend to be easier to paddle over long distances than shorter ones are (once you get them up to speed). They also stay on course better and hold more gear. Shorter kayaks weigh less, are less affected by winds, and are easier to maneuver and transport. However, they can be harder to paddle straight than longer kayaks.

The five primary types of kayaks are recreational kayaks, sit-on-top kayaks, inflatable kayaks, touring/sea kayaks, and river/whitewater kayaks.

Recreational Kayaks

Recreational kayaks are typically shorter, between 9 and 15 feet (2.7 and 4.6 m) long, with increased width that aids stability (see figure 5.9).

- *Advantages:* They have large open cockpits and more space for adaptation and are easy to enter and exit.
- *Disadvantages:* The large open space can make it difficult to provide sufficient support for those needing extensive seating adaptations.

Sit-on-Top Kayaks

Sit-on-top kayaks tend to have an average length and width and are reasonably stable.

- *Advantages:* Low or no sides make entry from land easy.
- *Disadvantages:* Reentry from the water is difficult for those who do not have full lower-limb function. The lack of a real cockpit can make it difficult to provide sufficient support for those needing extensive seating adaptations.

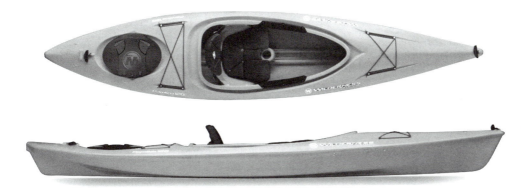

Figure 5.9
A recreational kayak.

Photos courtesy of
Wilderness Systems.

Inflatable Kayaks

These kayaks have average length with good stability but can be slower to paddle because of the soft hull.

- *Advantages:* Flexible sides can make entry and exit easy.
- *Disadvantages:* Reentry from the water is difficult for those who do not have full lower-limb function because the boat isn't a firm platform to pull against. The large open space is also challenging for extensive seating adaptations.

Touring/Sea Kayaks

Touring/sea kayaks are typically longer, narrower in width, and paddled more easily in a straight line (see figure 5.10) than other kayaks. Some have rudders or skegs (immovable rudders) that aid forward travel. Solo touring kayaks are typically 14 to 17 feet (4.3 to 5.2 m) long, and tandem kayaks (with two cockpits) are 18 feet (5.5 m) or longer.

- *Advantages:* In models with larger cockpits, entry and exit is easy and space is sufficient for a stable seat adaptation. These kayaks are very useful for paddlers who are unable to manage solo canoes, tire quickly, or have a significant loss of balance or vision.
- *Disadvantage:* Open-water paddling requires good instruction to understand efficient paddling, launching and landing techniques, safety and rescue techniques, tides, and navigation.

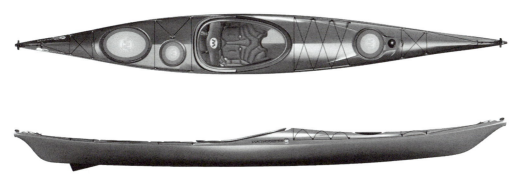

Figure 5.10
A touring/sea kayak.

Photos courtesy of
Wilderness Systems.

River/Whitewater Kayaks

These short boats are often barely longer than the paddler's legs, are usually initially stable, but can tip easily (see figure 5.11).

- *Advantages:* Their small size makes maneuvering the boat easier.
- *Disadvantages:* The small cockpit can make seating adaptation difficult. Instruction is necessary for learning maneuvers, rescues, river reading, and route finding.

Figure 5.11
A river/whitewater kayak.
Photos courtesy of Dagger.

Selecting a Paddle

Paddles are available in a variety of lengths, weights, materials, blade shapes, and blade angles. The choice of paddle might eliminate the need for an adaptation or make adaptation easier. For instance, shaft diameter can vary from slender to fatter to accommodate various hand sizes. Some paddlers will find a lighter-weight paddle easier to control without undue fatigue. A narrower blade can minimize fatigue and joint stress.

Canoeists use single-bladed paddles (see figure 5.12*a*); river kayakers use shorter, double-bladed paddles, which are different from the paddles sea kayakers use. Double-bladed paddles have flat or spoon-shaped blades. On double-bladed paddles, offset blades (oriented at different angles) are called "feathered" (see figure 5.12*b*); parallel blades (oriented at the same angle) are called "unfeathered" (see figure 5.12*c*).

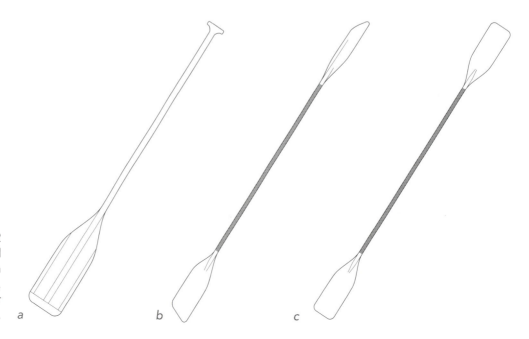

Figure 5.12
(a) A single-bladed paddle; *(b)* an offset, or feathered, blade; *(c)* parallel, or unfeathered, blades.

a   b   c

Good paddling technique increases stroke efficiency. Those who master torso rotation make good use of the large muscle groups, increase stroke power, and are less tired. Paddlers with disabilities should choose paddles that maximize their ability to paddle efficiently.

Remember the guiding principle for any paddle modification: Paddlers must be able to get their hands out of any paddle adaptation without assistance.

Consider the following when selecting a paddle:

Length   A longer paddle has many advantages:

- Extended reach for paddlers with limited range of motion.
- More efficient turning strokes for paddlers with less strength.
- Extended reach for paddlers seating on seats that have been lowered for greater stability.
- Extended reach for paddlers with limited use of their arms.
- More stability in bracing strokes for paddlers with decreased seating balance.

Be careful with kayak paddles longer than 220 cm, which can be unwieldy and diminish the advantages of greater leverage.

Weight   Lighter-weight paddles require less effort for

- paddlers with decreased arm strength or hand grip and
- paddlers who fatigue easily.

However, durable, lightweight paddles tend to be more expensive because of the materials used in their manufacture (carbon fiber, fiberglass).

Materials   Consider these advantages and disadvantages:

- Plastic and aluminum shafts can be difficult to grip when wet.
- Aluminum shafts can be cold to the hands in colder environments, thus decreasing circulation.
- Wood is warmer and more flexible than plastic and aluminum, and therefore reduces joint stress.

Design   These considerations can affect a person's performance:

- Paddles with longer shafts and smaller blades tend decrease the amount of effort needed to move them through the water. They can be helpful to paddlers with decreased range of motion, strength, and stamina.
- Paddles with larger-diameter shafts or ergonomically designed grips assist in paddlers' hand placement and clasping ability.
- Bent-shaft paddles can be used for ergonomic benefits but might be challenging to beginning paddlers or paddlers with limited range of motion.

Blade Angle for Double-Bladed Paddle   Decide whether a feathered or unfeathered blade is best. Feathered blades (offset angle) have less blade surface facing the wind, so there is less wind resistance for paddlers with decreased arm strength or hand grip. However, they require the rotation of one wrist.

Unfeathered blades (same angle) require no wrist rotation. Therefore, they require less effort for paddlers who fatigue easily, have decreased arm strength or hand grip, or decreased range of motion in the hand and wrist. However, more blade surface faces the wind, so there is more wind resistance.

If the paddler needs a hand adaptation to hold the paddle, the blade should be unfeathered. Break-apart, or sectional, paddles allow flexibility in feathering and unfeathering the paddle, but they can become loose over time and difficult to manipulate.

Hand Placement Paddlers who are weaker on one side than the other can change their hand placement with double-bladed paddles, moving the hand closer to the blade on the stronger side. This strategy keeps the boat tracking well because the stroke on the weaker side is now farther from the center of the boat and turns the boat back onto a straight course. The change in hand placement compensates for the overcorrecting effect of the stronger side.

Reference

American Canoe Association. (2004). *Critical judgment II: Understanding and preventing canoe and kayak fatalities*, 1996-2002. Springfield, VA: American Canoe Association.

PADDLER SAFETY CHECKLIST

This useful checklist can help prepare you and your participants for paddling experiences:

❏ *Be a swimmer.* Know the difference between, and when to use, aggressive and defensive swimming.

❏ *File a float plan.* Write down where you intend to put in and take out and when you expect to return. Give it to someone who will call for assistance if you don't return on time.

❏ *Wear a life jacket and keep it snug.* A properly fitting PFD extends below your rib cage, is buckled and zippered up snugly, and will not slide up and obscure your face when floating.

❏ *Assess your boat's flotation needs.* For flotation to work effectively, inflatable flotation bags and other types of flotation must fit snugly into the craft and be securely tied into place.

❏ *Carry a spare paddle.* You never know when you will break or lose a paddle.

❏ *Always dress for an unexpected flip.* The water is often colder than the air, and you lose body heat quickly if improperly dressed.

❏ *Wear a hat or helmet.* A helmet is important where upsets are likely or when using spray skirts or thigh restraints. A hat protects from the sun.

❏ *Bring a chart and compass or map of the river.* Know where you are and how to get out in an emergency.

❏ *Carry a whistle or sound signaling device.* The sound from such a device will carry across water and wind better than your voice.

❏ *Carry a light signal.* Devices such as strobes and flares are essential at night or on large bodies of water during emergencies.

❏ *Bring throw bags and other rescue gear.* Every group should be self-supporting and prepared to rescue its members.

❏ *Bring self-rescue devices such as paddle float, slings, and tow ropes.* Active self-rescue is essential, and it is the basis for all successful group rescues.

❏ *Carry a river knife.* You will need a knife when using ropes, throw bags, and rigging.

❏ *Have a bilge pump or bailer handy.* Those traveling in open water should always carry some device that can get water out of the boat.

❏ *Use sunscreen.* The glare from water increases sun exposure.

❏ *Use UV eye protection.* Choose a good pair of sunglasses and a strap.

❏ *Bring drinking water.* Dehydration leads to aching muscles, fatigue, and poor judgment.

❏ *Wear proper footwear.* Protect your feet from injury on lake and river shores.

❏ *Wear appropriate clothing.* Always dress for the weather and know what to expect. Temperature changes can occur rapidly. Layers of clothing insulate in cool weather better than a single garment.

❏ *Use a dry bag.* Dry clothing, cameras, and cell phones are great after a long day.

❏ *Carry a first aid kit with matches.* Carry supplies that match your level of first aid training.

❏ *Carry duct tape and a small repair kit.* A simple kit in a plastic bottle is easy to pack.

❏ *VHS radio and GPS locator.* If venturing away from shore in a coastal area, make sure you are able to call for rescue assistance if necessary.

From J. Zeller, 2009, *Canoeing and Kayaking for People With Disabilities* (Champaign, IL: Human Kinetics).

6

Disabilities and Their Implications for Paddling and Instruction

The purpose of this chapter is to provide a brief overview of various disabilities and their possible effect(s) on paddling, along with teaching suggestions pertinent to various functional impairments. Although every effort has been made to make this as comprehensive as possible, it is neither possible nor practical to cover all disabling conditions or diseases. Each person must be considered individually regardless of the particular disability because every person is affected differently.

For example, one person with multiple sclerosis may have minimal physical disabilities, and another person with the same disease may be unable to walk or sit unsupported. For this reason, this chapter describes the various disabilities in functional terms rather than medical terms as much as possible. See the glossary to clarify some commonly used medical terms.

A person may have a combination of functional impairments. For example, a person with quadriplegia may have various levels of loss of function in his or her legs, feet, trunk, hands, and arms. Read the information under each area that applies to that person's loss of function.

The following applies to *all* paddlers and will not be restated in subsequent sections:

- Teach a paddling technique that uses torso rotation. This method makes use of the large muscle groups, increases the efficiency of the stroke, and is less tiring.
- Encourage general paddling conditioning before the program.
- Allow ample time for rest, and set the pace of the trip appropriately.
- Encourage paddlers to be well rested and well fed.
- Encourage fluid intake because dehydration reduces paddlers' capacity to maintain top performance and increases fatigue.
- Share information about proper clothing before the program.
- Be prepared to use bracing strokes.
- Rolling is an important skill to learn to avoid unnecessary swims.

UPPER LIMB (ARM AND/OR HAND)

Commonly Related Conditions

arthritis, cerebral palsy, hemiplegia, quadriplegia, multiple sclerosis

Possible Implications for Paddling: Teaching Suggestions and Adaptations

Difficulty holding a paddle

- Have the paddler use a hand grip on the paddle (see hand grip adaptations, p. 85, in chapter 8).

Lack of strength

- Have the paddler keep the paddle low to the boat while paddling.
- Have the paddler try a double-bladed paddle.
- A paddler with reduced function in the triceps can pull the paddle even though pushing with the opposite hand may be difficult.
- Teach the paddler to pull the blade slowly because pulling is easier when less turbulence is created.

Lack of control of paddle movements (e.g., tremors)

- Weighted wrist cuffs, heavier paddles, or both, may help to decrease hand tremor, but they also increase the effort required to move the paddle.
- Consider having the paddler use either a right-hand or left-hand controlled, double-bladed paddle depending on which side is stronger and has more control.

Range of motion affected

- Consider having the paddler use an unfeathered kayak paddle or a 70-degree blade angle instead of a 90-degree feather. A reduced blade angle requires less wrist torque.
- Have the paddler use a paddle with a smaller blade area for either canoeing or kayaking because a large blade area requires more strength to use.

Swimming ability affected

- Thoroughly evaluate the person's swimming ability and possibly recommend a higher-flotation life jacket or type I device (see Life Jackets or Personal Flotation Devices [PFDs] in chapter 5, p. 34).
- Recommend that the student take an adapted aquatics class, if possible, before beginning instruction.

Easily fatigued

- Consider having the person use a lighter-weight paddle and boat.

Difficulty entering and exiting the boat

- Be ready to provide additional support to compensate for loss of balance.
- Have the person practice wet exits in a pool.

Difficulty carrying the boat

- Use boat-carrying carts and scout for an easy put-in, or launching, site that does not require as much carrying.

Susceptible to cold or heat

- Make sure the person is prepared for the weather and water conditions by wearing proper clothing (see Selecting Clothing, p. 31, in chapter 5).

Possible Implications for Paddling:
Teaching Suggestions and Adaptations

Damaged or wet prosthesis

- Suggest that the person use a prosthesis designed for use in water, because other designs could be damaged. In addition, a waterlogged device can negatively affect the paddler's balance and swimming ability.

- If a prosthesis is not designed for water use, develop an adaptation for the person when he is not wearing it. Have the person bring the prosthesis along to use when on land. Keep it securely attached to the boat inside a waterproof container, or transport it by shuttle vehicle to the takeout point.

- If the prosthesis is designed for water use but keeps slipping off the residual limb, use a medium or small neoprene knee brace large enough to go over the prosthetic and the bicep, anchoring the prosthesis while still allowing the person to remove it in an emergency.

- Adapt paddling clothing to allow for the emergency removal of a prosthesis. Dry tops and splash tops that fit snugly over the wrist of a prosthesis trap the prosthesis to the wearer, thus preventing an escape if that arm is caught. The person should use short dry tops and splash guards or adapt the sleeve and wrist closure of a long-sleeved top.

Limb prone to injury if unprotected

- Make sure the person wears protection over the exposed residual limb. Each person will have unique tissue sensitivity issues. Discuss with the person the potential skin injury danger and develop protective or padded barriers accordingly.

Difficulty holding a paddle

- Either modify the paddle or use an attachment system if the paddler is using a waterproof prosthesis to allow an adequate paddle grip. The person must be able to immediately and independently release the prosthesis from the paddle or attachment system if necessary. Before allowing a paddler to use such an adaptation on a river or open water, test it during a wet exit in a controlled environment with clear, calm water so you can see the underwater action clearly. Other people in the water must be ready to assist if the paddler has any difficulties independently releasing the paddle during this practice. If assistance is necessary, modify the adaptation and retest it to ensure that the paddler can independently release the paddle.

- Wet exit technique for use by a single-sided hand, below-elbow (BE), or above-elbow (AE) amputee. The uninjured arm is used to releasing the kayak spray skirt from the cockpit combing. As the paddler's legs clear the kayak, the paddler should release the terminal device from the paddle shaft using the uninjured hand because the paddle represents a big entrapment danger. The person then tucks the paddle under the residual limb and uses the uninjured arm to swim and catch an assist from another kayak.

- Have the person use an adapted style of paddling.

- In the bow of a canoe, the paddler could use a single-bladed adapted paddle with the residual arm. The stern paddler could use a double-bladed paddle, if necessary, to compensate.

Swimming ability affected by the absence of a limb

- The person's PFD must provide adequate flotation and fit securely.

- The person should first try swimming with a PFD in a safe environment.

- If planning whitewater or surf or sea kayaking, have the paddler swim either a Class I rapid or swim through the surf line wearing full paddling gear to give both the paddler and the potential rescuer an idea of the effort required.

With a high amputation, difficulty keeping the PFD on when swimming

- Have the person use a correctly sized type III PFD that fits appropriately and ensure that the adjustment tabs are pulled snuggly and all clips are fastened. See Life Jackets or Personal Flotation Devices (PFDs) on page 34 in chapter 5 for tips on how to fit the PFD. Be sure the PFD is tight enough that it can't slide above the paddler's head when afloat.

Commonly Related Conditions

cerebral palsy, paraplegia, quadriplegia (affecting trunk balance)

Possible Implications for Paddling:
Teaching Suggestions and Adaptations

Difficulty sitting unsupported

- Seat needs to be modified (see Adaptation Principles in chapter 7).
- Back support is necessary; lateral support at the sides of the paddler's chest may also be needed.
- Always allow for easy exit from the boat.
- Never use Velcro, chest straps, or any products or techniques that bind the paddler to the craft or paddle.

Difficulty performing some strokes

- Teach a variety of strokes.
- Have the paddler try a double-bladed paddle in a canoe because the grip may be easier to adapt for certain hand disabilities than the shaft of a canoe paddle.
- Adapt the paddle (see hand grip adaptations, p. 85, in chapter 8).

Balance affected; balance affects boat lean or trim

- In a canoe, lowering the seat 1 to 4 inches (2.5 to 10 cm) may be helpful to improve balance; however, sitting on the canoe floor decreases stroke efficiency.
- In a kayak, add enough padding on the seat to protect the person against pressure sores, but keep in mind that a higher center of gravity reduces stability.
- Paddlers must have their weight distributed evenly (boat trim), so as not to affect boat direction. They may not be aware that weight has shifted to one side. Paddling companions can watch for uneven weight distribution.
- Have the person use a tandem kayak or canoe, so a partner can help with balance.
- Bracing strokes are essential; have the person practice them while you support the paddle.
- Video recordings are helpful for showing paddlers how they are leaning the boats as well as other aspects of their paddling technique.

Susceptible to temperature changes

- Make sure the person wears proper clothing (see Selecting Clothing, p. 31, in chapter 5).
- Have the person take more frequent breaks for food intake or hydration if necessary.

Difficulty entering and exiting the boat

- Have the person practice wet exits.
- Be ready to provide support for balance.

GENERAL IMPAIRMENT OF THE LEG(S)

Commonly Related Conditions

arthritis, phlebitis

Possible Implications for Paddling:
Teaching Suggestions and Adaptations

Difficulty kneeling in the canoe or sitting in a canoe or kayak

- Provide a seat support system to maximize stability (see Adaptation Principles, chapter 7, and various types of seat adaptations, p. 96, in chapter 8).
- Consider lowering the seat slightly to lower the center of gravity, or add back and side supports.

Decreased sensation and circulation; prone to skin abrasion and bruising

- Provide seating with adequate cushioning.
- Be alert to the risk of hypothermia or heat exhaustion.
- Have the person wear proper clothing (see Selecting Clothing, p. 31, in chapter 5).
- If circulation is decreased, do not have the person kneel because it would further impair circulation.
- Check the boat interior for sharp or rough areas. Remove or pad those areas.

LOWER LIMB (LEG AND/OR FOOT): PEOPLE USING WHEELCHAIRS

Commonly Related Conditions

paraplegia, quadriplegia, muscular dystrophy, hemiplegia

Possible Implications for Paddling: Teaching Suggestions and Adaptations

Difficulty entering and exiting the boat

- When transferring a person from a wheelchair to a canoe or kayak, have the boat at the water's edge because the seat heights are more equal. Once the person is in the boat, slide the boat into the water.

- If it is necessary to transfer from a dock or pool deck to a floating boat, a person may be able to transfer from the wheelchair directly to the dock or pool deck and then into the boat. The boat must be held steady. Place padding on the dock or pool deck where the paddler will be seated, even briefly.

- When the boat is stable at the water's edge, a person may be able to position the wheelchair next to it and transfer directly into the boat.

- A midpoint transfer may be helpful. Place a cooler or overturned milk crate between the wheelchair and the boat. Place padding on the top. Transfer the person from the wheelchair to the midpoint and then to the boat. Reverse the transfer process when the person is exiting the boat. When the transfer is divided into two parts, the total height of each transfer is more manageable.

- When the boat is on the dock, a person can transfer into the boat, and then the boat and paddler can be placed in the water.

Individuals know the best way to transfer themselves. Discuss the transfer with the student and then use this information to determine the safest place to complete the transfer. Ask for directions from the student and offer assistance—for example: "I am willing to help. Tell me what to do if you want my help." If the student agrees to assistance, ask where you should place your hands. People unable to transfer independently can direct others as to the amount and type of assistance required. Take care not to injure yourself, especially your back, during this process. When lifting, always bend at the knees and keep the lower back straight, using leg strength, not back strength.

Special appliances (e.g., a catheter and leg bag or colostomy appliance)

- Carefully transfer from a wheelchair to a boat to make sure that special appliances are not moved out of place. Check with the person as to hand placement.

- In the pool ensure that the appliance is protected, especially during wet exits and reentries. If the leg bag or colostomy bag were to become disconnected, the person would be highly susceptible to infection from the pool water. The pool would likely have to be closed and drained as a result of contamination from the bag contents.

Difficulty sitting stably

- Sliding in the boat seat while paddling affects balance and makes paddle strokes less effective.

- The person should be secure in the seat but still be able to exit freely. Make adaptations to the seat and the area around the seat (see Keep It Safe, p. 68, in chapter 7).

- An upward angle at the front seat edge will aid in preventing paddlers from sliding forward in their seats (see Stable Seating, p. 70, in chapter 7).

- Legs need to be placed evenly in the boat. Often when the boat leans, the leg on the high side may shift to the low side and affect balance.
- Design and place padding between the legs to keep them separated. Be sure that this padding does not hinder exits.

Concern for wheelchair security

- Paddlers may be concerned about their wheelchairs' security if left on shore. They may want to bring the chairs if the group will be landing somewhere during the paddle. A manual, folding wheelchair can be brought in a canoe. A battery-powered wheelchair would need to be transported in a vehicle.
- A wheelchair should be placed in a secure location; a locked vehicle is best. Be sure other people will not sit in it, play with it, or otherwise disturb it.

Difficulty exiting from a boat in the event of a capsize

- Remove the foot pegs from a kayak to avoid foot entrapment or injury.
- In a canoe, do not place the paddler's legs under a thwart where they may be pinned during a capsize.
- When using seating adaptations, check for easy exit.

Decreased sensation and circulation; prone to skin abrasion and bruising

- Pad with closed-cell foam to protect any areas where skin without sensation will come in contact with any hard surface. Without sensation, paddlers may be unaware that they are being injured (see Skin Protection, p. 74, in chapter 7 and Appendix D on p. 131).
- Padding on the bottom of a kayak will also help insulate the legs from the cooling effects of water beneath the boat.
- Too much padding affects the boat's balance because it raises the paddler's center of gravity.
- Foot protection and long pants provide extra skin protection.
- The paddler may need to check the skin for pressure points caused by prolonged sitting in one position without adequate cushioning.
- For paddlers susceptible to skin breakdown, it is important to keep the skin as dry as possible.
- Avoid having sensitive skin stay wet for a long time because skin may break down more quickly when wet.
- Avoid a tight grasp on the body when assisting with transfers between a wheelchair and a boat because bruising may result.
- See appendix D for more information on skin breakdown issues.

Increased susceptibility to temperature variations

- With a spinal cord injury or disease, the body's temperature control mechanism may be disrupted. Hypothermia and heat exhaustion may occur more quickly. Shivering and sweating may be absent below the level of the injury, so an increased awareness of temperature and its effect on the paddler is needed.
- Check the weather and water temperature. Plan for temperature extremes (hot or cold). Remember that the weather may change, the wind may rise, or a storm may move in during the day. Be prepared.
- Pay attention to clothing: Have paddlers use dry suits, wet suits, synthetics, or wool and dress in layers for warmth. Prepare for a variety of water and wind temperatures. Paddlers should bring one or two dry changes of clothes to prepare for a possible capsize.

- A vest instead of a Farmer John–style wet suit is recommended, because the latter is difficult to get on and may constrict a catheter or leg bag. Instead, the person can use wet suit booties and a layering system on the legs.

- A barrier (wet suit or dry suit) is the only system that will aid in retaining body heat when the paddler is in the water. (See Selecting Clothing, on p. 31, in chapter 5.)

- Handling anyone with hypothermia requires a quick response. Rewarming should be done carefully. Consult general outdoor texts or emergency manuals for more detailed information on hypothermia if you are not familiar with signs, symptoms, and treatment of the different stages.

- Rewarm areas with normal sensation first and slowly. For example, when warming a person with a lack of sensation in the legs, warm the torso first. If a person lacks sensation on one side of the body, first warm the side with normal sensation.

Caution: For paddlers with no sensation, avoid skin exposure to extremely warm surfaces because the paddler could be burned without feeling the heat. If skin is fragile, extremes in the temperature of surfaces against the skin will be harmful.

Sudden muscle spasms affecting balance

- Cold water, overexertion, sudden motion, and improper seating may cause an increase in spasticity. Avoid these if possible.

Legs drag or float due to a loss of muscle mass

- Ask the person if her legs tend to drag when she is in the water. On rivers it may be safer to float rapids on her back with the body and legs sideways to the river. This position helps to prevent the legs and feet from becoming entangled in obstacles, but it leaves the swimmer at great risk with no buffer for her head. Paddlers should always practice swimming rapids in controlled conditions.

- It is always preferable to swim rapids feet first. A wet suit or a ring of closed-cell foam secured at the ankles will help the legs float and allow swimming in the safer feet first position. Such precautions must be taken before they are needed.

LOWER-LIMB AMPUTATION

Possible Implications for Paddling:
Teaching Suggestions and Adaptations

If considering the use of a lower-limb prosthesis while paddling, careful evaluation is essential

- In a decked boat, a lower-limb prosthesis could become wedged during a capsize and cause entrapment. It is strongly recommended that a person *not* wear a lower-limb prosthesis in a closed-deck boat. The potential for entrapment, or at the least significant encumbrance, during a wet exit is very high as is the risk of losing a $50,000 prosthesis once wet.
- If the boat type poses an entrapment potential or the paddler's prosthesis is not designed for water use, develop an adaptation for the paddler when not wearing the prosthesis. (See Functional Impairment Lower-Limb Amputation, p. 98, in chapter 8.) Bring it along to use when on land. Either secure the prosthesis in a waterproof container attached to an open boat, or transport it by shuttle vehicle to the takeout point.
- If using a closed-deck boat, transport the prosthesis by shuttle vehicle to the takeout point. An above-the-knee (AK) prosthesis will not fit in a closed-deck boat with an able-bodied paddler or ride safely in an amputee's boat.

Damaged or wet prosthesis

- A prosthesis not designed for use in water could be damaged during paddling. In addition, a waterlogged prosthesis would negatively affect the paddler's balance and swimming ability.
- If you decide that the person can safely wear a prosthesis in a boat (other than a closed-deck boat), have him use only a device designed for use in water.
- If the paddler's prosthesis is not designed for use in water, develop an adaptation for the person without it. Follow the advice in the preceding section for transporting the device.
- In a closed-deck boat, have the prosthesis waiting at the takeout point.

Limb prone to injury if unprotected

- Paddlers should wear protection over exposed residual limbs. Each person will have unique tissue sensitivity issues; discuss with the student the potential skin injury danger, and develop protective barriers accordingly.

Swimming ability affected by the absence of a limb

- The person's life jacket must provide adequate flotation and fit securely.
- The person should first try swimming with the life jacket in a safe environment.
- If planning whitewater or surf or sea kayaking, have the paddler swim either a Class I rapid or swim through the surf line with full gear to give both the paddler and the potential rescuer an idea of the effort required.

Difficulty entering and exiting the boat

- If the person requires assistance getting into and out of the boat, discuss and practice strategies in a stable environment.

Difficulty sitting stably

- The person must be secure in the seat and still be able to exit freely. (See Adaptation Principles, chapter 7).

- A holder can be built into the craft to protect the residual limb and to prevent the person from sliding in the seat. The holder can be made using Ethafoam padded with closed-cell foam.
- Compensate for lower-limb weight loss by adding ballast to the boat. (See Ballast, p. 96, in chapter 8.)

Difficulty kneeling in the canoe or sitting in a canoe or kayak

- Provide a bracing point to maximize stability. (See Adaptations, p. 98.)
- Consider lowering the seat slightly to lower the center of gravity or add back and side supports.

Decreased sensation and circulation; prone to skin abrasion and bruising

- Check the boat interior for sharp or rough areas. Remove or pad those areas.
- Provide adequate cushioning.
- If circulation is decreased, do not allow the person to kneel because doing so would further impair circulation.

HEARING IMPAIRMENT

Possible Implications for Paddling: Teaching Suggestions and Adaptations

Difficulty with on-water communication

- Practice signals to be used with all participants before they are needed.
- Simple signals are best. (See On-Water Communication, p. 57.)
- A bright orange flag could be used to draw attention to the signaler.
- Other paddlers must be observant because the person with a hearing impairment may not be able to hear an emergency whistle.
- Keep the same paddling partners together to facilitate the development of signs and other communication techniques. Choose a paddling partner for the person with a hearing impairment who is easy to lip read and who enunciates clearly.

Difficulty hearing the instructions or unable to hear them at all

- Speak and look directly at the person.
- Speak clearly and distinctly, using normal tones. Shouting makes it harder to lip read.
- Mustaches may hinder lip reading.
- Make sure the person has visual contact with you during instructional sessions.
- Demonstrations are valuable. If possible, begin instruction in a controlled setting (e.g., pool deck or pool), so that you can stand behind the student or in the pool and physically manipulate the student's paddle.
- Be sure the sun is not at your back when speaking.
- Use pen and paper to facilitate communication, if necessary. Special pens that can be used when wet are available from camping goods stores. You can also use wipe-off communication boards (such as those used in scuba).
- Explain the intended route by drawing directions in the sand.
- If a person who is hearing impaired is with an interpreter, direct your conversation to the person and not to the interpreter. (For example, say, "Hold the paddle at this angle" rather than, "Tell him to hold the paddle at this angle.")
- Check to be sure the person has understood the instructions by asking a direct question that requires an answer that summarizes the instruction.
- A person with a hearing impairment should not be in the bow or lead boat. Canoeing in the stern seat allows a paddler to see hand signals from the bow paddler.
- When paddling tandem, tapping on the canoe so the paddler with the hearing impairment can feel the vibration is a good method to get attention.

Balance affected

- Lower the student's center of gravity in the boat—for example, lower the seat or suggest that the person kneel in a canoe instead of sit.

Hearing aid damaged by water

- Students must be informed of the potential risk to their equipment.
- Consider having the person carry her hearing aid and batteries in a waterproof bag secured to the boat or in her vest pocket.

Difficulty communicating during a rescue

- Practice rescues in a safe environment before going on the open water.
- Students should use a U.S. Coast Guard whistle in an emergency even if they cannot hear it. Try the loud, high-pitched whistle during rescue practice, because a person who has some loss of hearing may be able to hear it.

On-Water Communication

Communication on the water is necessary when there is an emergency or when routine information needs to be shared with other paddlers in the group. Prior to departure, review the signals clearly with everyone in the group.

The following general guidelines apply:

- Do not depend on voice commands.
- Simple is best in signals. The purpose is to attract attention.
- Hand and paddle signals can be used on rivers.
- Plan a backup system to use if the first signal does not attract attention.
- All paddlers should have a U.S. Coast Guard–approved waterproof signal whistle attached to their PFDs.
- Whistles should be used only for emergencies.

On the river, the American Whitewater Universal River Signals (see appendix F) are useful. However, they do not work if other paddlers are not looking or cannot see across large bodies of water.

If the group includes a paddler who is hearing or visually impaired, adapt the signal system. Show that paddler the illustrations in advance of being on the water, and ask him which ones would be most helpful and what changes are needed to catch his attention. For example, use a bright orange flag signal for a paddler who is hearing impaired or a clanging device for a paddler who is visually impaired.

With greater distances, visibility may be difficult. Bright-colored life jackets, helmets, boat decks, paddle blades, and reflecting tape increase visibility. Handheld flares are effective. Sea kayaking books and resources often contain extensive information on signaling devices for open-water paddling.

Sound may not carry in certain water and weather conditions. Open-water paddling (lakes and oceans) requires additional signaling techniques. Canister air horns are good backup signaling systems.

VISUAL IMPAIRMENT

Possible Implications for Paddling:
Teaching Suggestions and Adaptations

Determine level of function

- Ask a student who has some loss of vision, "What can you see?"

- Ask a student who has very limited vision or is blind, "How do you generally learn how to do new things?" Similar methods might be applicable to paddling instruction.

Must wear glasses to see clearly

- Have the paddler use eyeglass holders (e.g., Chubs and Croakies). The person should also bring extra glasses or contacts in a secure container.

Difficulty following the outlined course (e.g., sighting)

- Consider pairing the person who is visually impaired with a person who is not visually impaired, so the person can give verbal instructions and can describe the physical environment, such as a bend in the river.

- Directions such as *right/left* or *port/starboard* work well with some people.

- Suggest using another stroke. In tandem boats, the paddler with full vision could tell a partner to draw harder or forward sweep. A simple command, such as *change*, can be used to have the person change paddling sides.

Difficulty benefiting fully from visual demonstrations

- When teaching people with a visual impairment in a group situation, use names so they are aware they are being addressed.

- Give explicit verbal instructions.

- After explaining to the student what you are going to do, hold the student's hands on the paddle to demonstrate strokes.

- When appropriate, try to make use of residual vision or memories of visual images. Try to make comparisons between the strokes and familiar actions. For instance, the pushing and pulling motions used when sweeping the floor can be compared to the arm motions used in the forward and sweep strokes.

- Use the clock method for directions (straight in front of the person is 12:00 and directly behind is 6:00). For instance, you could tell the student to use the draw stroke at 2:00.

- Use tactile models. A small model river can be constructed on the floor using rescue ropes for the riverbanks, small rocks, and a scale model canoe or kayak. The student can feel the curve of the shoreline as you explain the area of stronger currents on an outside curve, boat angle for ferrying, and the flow of water around the rocks to create eddies. Tactile models are visually helpful for other students as well.

- Check to be sure the person has understood your instructions.

- Try to avoid chatter, as it tends to be distracting.

Difficulty with on-water communication

- Practice signals with all participants before they are needed.

- A clanging device can be used for various signals, such as to gather for lunch.

- A whistle should be used only for emergencies.

Difficult seeing boats during a rescue

- Practice rescues before going on the open water.
- In whitewater, have the person feel the water to understand river currents. Place his hand, arm, or paddle in the water or have him wade into a shallow section. The paddler must understand water currents to know how they will push the boat. Help him feel the main downstream current and eddies where water moves upstream.
- Have the paddler practice swimming rapids with a buddy in safe areas.

Difficulty determining which stroke to use

- In a tandem boat, a paddler with full vision could tell a partner with a visual impairment to draw or draw harder or forward sweep. Paddling partners can agree on simple commands, such as *hut* to change paddling sides.

LUNG DISEASES

Commonly Related Conditions

asthma, emphysema, or any neurological or muscular disorder impairing the respiratory muscles

Possible Implications for Paddling: Teaching Suggestions and Adaptations

Shortness of breath and wheezing

- A person with a chronic breathing impairment may have an inhaler or other medicine. Have the person keep an extra inhaler or medicine handy and stored in a waterproof container that is tied to the boat or in a PFD pocket.

- Shortness of breath may be brought on by overexertion, stress, high altitude, air temperature, or air quality. Be aware of these causes and be alert to preliminary symptoms. Early intervention is important. High pollen counts can irritate bronchial tubes and exacerbate an asthma attack.

- Watch for signs of labored breathing and encourage the person to rest before continuing.

- Supplemental breathing equipment, including oxygen tanks, can easily be carried in an open canoe in a waterproof container. Breathing equipment should be secured in the canoe to avoid weight shift or a capsize.

Easily fatigued

- Watch for signs of fatigue and set the pace of the trip accordingly.

- Consider pairing the paddler with a lung disease with a strong partner.

- Rest after an attack until the person is ready to continue.

- Check the person's swimming ability. Consider having the person use a type I, or more buoyant, PFD (see Life Jackets or Personal Flotation Devices [PFDs], p. 34, in chapter 5).

Difficulty assisting in a rescue

- As a result of shortness of breath or fatigue during the rescue process, the paddler may need to be coached more fully and calmed during a rescue.

- Practice rescues.

COGNITIVE AND BRAIN FUNCTION IMPAIRMENT

Possible Implications for Paddling: Teaching Suggestions and Adaptations

Although labels vary, a number of disabilities have some behavioral implications—particularly, traumatic brain injury (TBI), attention-deficit/hyperactivity disorder (ADHD), stroke, dyslexia, and cognitive developmental disability. Brain-based behaviors that are pertinent particularly to individuals with TBI are marked with an asterisk in the following list. Such behaviors may be the result of other conditions, however, particularly when learning new skills such as paddling.

Fatigues easily*

- Profound fatigue affects a paddler's ability to maintain balance, slows verbal and motor response time, and delays verbal and motor responses.
- Plan adaptations if you anticipate rapid development of fatigue (even if initial balance and skill efficiency is not a noticeable issue).
- Have a backup plan for when a student becomes fatigued, such as slowing the pace or shortening the trip.
- Design shorter instructional periods followed by reviews.
- Build rest periods into the lesson.
- Plan more strenuous or physically demanding skills—rescues, wet exits, and boat reentries—for a time that can be followed by a rest period.
- Have the person paddle in a tandem boat.

Lack of awareness of physical needs (thirst, discomfort)

- If the student is unable to convey needs, check for subtle signs and ask questions.
- Remind the person to drink fluids frequently.

Impulsiveness in motor and verbal responses*

- Use a buddy system—pair an experienced paddler with a new student.
- Use tandem boats if possible.
- Establish a stop signal so students can be cued when they become impulsive.
- Use a partner (other than the paddling partner) who can provide visual and verbal prompts as needed to redirect behavior or help the person following directions.
- Use the person's name and make eye contact when redirecting behavior.
- Use smaller instructor/student ratios in supervision (sometimes one-on-one instruction is needed).

Speech slow and delayed in conversation or verbal responses; may repeat self frequently*

- Allow sufficient wait time for responses.
- Establish a signal to cue the student that he is repeating himself.
- Consider a smaller instructor/student ratio.
- Present information in short, concise chunks.
- Check for understanding frequently.

Difficulty following multistep directions and processing information to learn skills

- Keep directions simple and concise; don't use jargon or complex terminology when simpler words will suffice.

- Reduce teaching to basic concrete teaching points, using mnemonics (memory assists such as "loose hips save ships"), props, visuals, or a few key points when possible.
- Check for understanding of instructions by asking key questions or seeking verbal responses to a few key points.
- Use acronyms or one-word prompts that are easy to remember (e.g., CPR for "catch, power, recovery" to teach a stroke).
- Use shorter teaching sequences: Break each skill into only three parts or teach only three parts of the skill at a time followed by repeated practice.
- Teach at a slower pace.
- Consider a smaller instructor/student ratio.
- Use a practical demonstration with your hand over the paddler's hand if needed.
- Make sure the student can demonstrate each skill before moving on to the next one.
- Repeat, repeat, repeat the skill and demo sequence as needed!
- Build on previous skills and relate the skill being taught to something the person knows when possible.
- Use colored tape on the power face or back face of the paddle to orient the person to the correct blade position in water.
- Use colored tape on the paddle as a visual prompt for correct hand placement.
- Make a laminated picture of a boat or paddle with labels for the student to refer to during class.
- Use strips of contrasting colored tape on the gunwales of tandem canoes or the decks of tandem kayaks to orient students to the proper paddling side (e.g., mark the port/bow and starboard/stern sides of the canoe in yellow tape, so partners paddle on the opposite yellow sides; mark the port bow and stern of the kayak in yellow tape so partners paddle in sync on the same side).
- Mark the gunwale or the deck of the boat with contrasting tape to show where the person should begin and end the stroke—for example, from the green to red tape marks.
- For more autonomy, have the person choose the color(s) of tape to use.
- Give praise and encouragement for correct performance and verbal responses.
- Do not switch boats or paddles or teach in a different place during the course of the lesson. It may be confusing to the student.

Poor judgment or inappropriate behavior

- Use a smaller instructor/student ratio for supervision.
- Use stop signals and redirection; see the preceding discussion of impulsiveness.

POSTTRAUMATIC STRESS DISORDER (PTSD)

Possible Implications for Paddling: Teaching Suggestions and Adaptations

Some people who experience very traumatic events end up with ongoing psychological problems related to their trauma. Soldiers who are exposed to combat are at risk for ongoing difficulties, but a majority of combat veterans do not develop persistent problems. If symptoms do cause problems in the person's life, he might have posttraumatic stress disorder (PTSD). Individuals with PTSD present a wide variety of symptoms and cope with their illness in a variety of ways. Individuals with PTSD might identify their illness, or they may remain private about it. In the military culture, soldiers are discouraged from revealing weaknesses or mental illness, and veterans are often hesitant to expose this kind of information even years after leaving the military. The following suggestions could apply in either situation.

Individuals with PTSD experience four types of symptoms, which you may encounter during paddling instruction or a trip.

Replaying Upsetting Events

If a student encounters upsetting memories, he could become extremely upset in a way that is not related to the current experience. Individuals with PTSD sometimes have physical symptoms (increased heart rate, dizziness, rapid breathing) when reminded of their trauma. It is possible that the trigger for the reaction can be easily identified, although sometimes it comes out of nowhere. Some people can be triggered by a feeling, and learning to paddle can involve feelings of helplessness, fear, excitement, and trust—all of which can trigger traumatic memories. An extreme replay of trauma is called a flashback; although very uncommon, they can be very upsetting and disorienting.

Approaches

- Remind the person who she is and who the people surrounding her are, tell her she is safe, and ask if she needs time to recover.

- It could also be helpful to ask the person if there are things he has done in the past to help him cope with such memories.

- Encourage the person to do whatever needs to be done at her own pace and explain that the class does not need to move forward beyond her comfort level.

- Because some people receive a great deal of support from other survivors of similar trauma, you can ask if it would be helpful to have another student with a similar background to provide encouragement or guidance.

Avoiding Triggers

Individuals with PTSD sometimes try to avoid any experiences that could remind them of their past. This avoidance can be very specific to the ingredients of their trauma, or it can be very general, including types of people, feelings in relationships, or kinds of activities. Avoidance can be very obvious, such as not reading the news; it can also be very subtle, such as a feeling of detachment from other people. Paddling can be a trigger because of the trust required, physical risk, canoe partners, and other unknown reasons. A student could experience an unexpected trigger during a session and never return. If the trigger is understood and addressed adequately, the student could be encouraged to continue participation.

Approaches

- Avoidance is a very reasonable response to upsetting events. It is important to help the student understand that avoidance is normal and its function is to protect him.

- Remember that PTSD is different from normal anxiety about drowning; it is linked to a past experience and can show up in very surprising ways. You might never know what sparked the reaction, including simple statements such as: "Staying away from dangerous things has protected humans for thousands of years. Let's look at what we are doing right now to make this situation as safe as possible." Looking at photos, videos, and demonstrations by other paddlers can all be helpful steps in moving the person forward in overcoming avoidance.

- Every small effort to face a fear should be noted and encouraged: "You made it through that; it seemed to take a lot. Are you ready for the next challenge, or do you want to take a break?"

- It is inadvisable to push people to experience the elements they are avoiding without sufficient preparation and overt agreement. Again, another student's encouragement or the opportunity to encourage someone else can greatly help a student overcome this kind of avoidance.

Being Easily Startled or on Guard

Some people who have experienced trauma show a high level of jumpiness or a strong startle reflex when surprised. They sometimes "take cover" when they hear a loud noise or go into a defense mode in a situation in which you would not expect it. The other common symptom is to be very mistrustful and guarded about personal safety. This can manifest as obvious fearfulness, distractibility, or irritability.

Approaches

- As with avoidance, it is important to normalize the response and prevent the student from being so embarrassed that he leaves the class. Often the shame attached to overreacting in a social situation is so great that a person with PTSD will become increasingly isolated for fear of reexperiencing such a situation in public.

- Because another student's input can sometimes save the day, consider encouraging interaction between students.

- Preventing unexpected loud noises and other surprises is a good idea, but it is impossible to stop them altogether.

- Make a point to prepare the entire group for the kinds of events you may encounter, such as the possibility other groups will cross your route, a paddler may capsize, the paddle route passes by a noisy area where communication may be difficult, and so on. Discuss how they will be addressed if they come up.

- Monitor the student for clues that he is becoming detached, irritable, or on guard. Should you notice this in the early stages, take time to identify the specific aspects of the situation and walk through the student's usual coping mechanism for each one. If the person has a strong reaction to a trigger, do your best to avoid embarrassing him and give him an opportunity to recover a sense of safety before forging ahead.

Difficulty Dealing With Large Groups, Authority Figures, High Distraction, and Stimulation

Individuals with PTSD often don't deal well with big groups, high-pressure authority, or distracting or overly stimulating environments.

Approaches

- Organize small groups for instruction and paddling trips.

- Develop mutual goals and work calmly toward them as a group rather than in deference to the instructor or trip leader.

- Select settings for instruction or trips that are free of distraction or stimulation.

Possible Implications for Paddling:
Teaching Suggestions and Adaptations

Check with the student during the paddler's interview about the side effects of any medicine related to sun, exertion, and other factors in the outdoor environment, if medications are listed but no side effects are noted on the medical information sheet.

Body temperature and its regulating mechanisms may be affected.

- Check weather and water temperatures. Have the person wear appropriate layers of clothing. (See Selecting Clothing, p. 31, in chapter 5.)

Severe dehydration as a result of taking psychotropic medications

- Have the person increase fluid intake.

Increased sensitivity to sunlight

- Some drugs such as phenothiazines, Bactrim, tetracycline, and psychotropic medicines result in hypersensitivity to the sun. People taking these drugs burn easily. It is essential that paddlers know whether the medications they take increase sun sensitivity. Medications can be checked with the person who takes them, a physician, or pharmacist.

Caution: People who are allergic to sulfa drugs may react to sunscreens with the ingredient PABA in them.

Reflection is heightened on the water

- Paddlers should use sun visors, sunblock, or zinc oxide.
- Paddlers should apply waterproof sunscreen with a minimum protection of SPF 15 on all exposed body parts.
- Paddlers should apply sunscreen after getting wet or splashing.
- Encourage paddlers to wear white or light-colored clothing.
- Lightweight, long-sleeved shirts and long pants also provide protection.
- Wetting and wearing hats or bandannas will keep paddlers cool.
- Hats with wide brims can protect the face from the sun. However, they may hold heat and should not be used if the person is very sensitive to the heat.
- Avoid paddling, if possible, during the prime sun hours of noon to 4 p.m.

7

Adaptation Principles

Most paddlers select paddles and boats based on performance features and comfort, and then they make some modifications to their boats' seating areas to maximize performance. Adapting a boat or paddle to compensate for loss of function due to a disability is really no different. A basic guideline is keeping it as simple as possible.

By simply changing the style of a boat or paddle, you may be able to solve a boating problem for a person with a disability without the need to make equipment adaptations. However, if an adaptation is necessary to compensate for a loss of function, seating stability, or skin protection needs, keep the following principles in mind:

1. Learn from the paddler with a disability.

   o Discuss and apply the adaptation process with the student paddler for whom the adaptation is intended. When you first learn about a student's disability, you can use the manual to determine several possible adaptations, but wait to make final decisions until you are with the student. When evaluating the options, the student can best tell you what is helpful and what is not and how tweaks to the adaptation can improve the fit.

   o Leverage ideas from other adaptations the student is using in sports or daily life. Sometimes solutions that work for other activities can be adapted or provide an idea for a boating-specific solution.

   o Once the adaptation is ready for use, observe the paddler using the adaptation on water and look for indicators that the paddler is sliding in the seat or compensating for inadequacies in the adaptation. Discuss how the adaptation is working out and change or optimize the adaptation if necessary.

2. Keep it simple.

   o Use as much standard equipment as possible. The more complicated a system is, the more likely it is that something will go wrong.

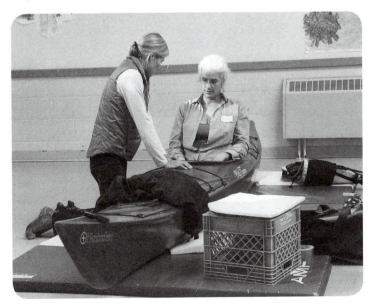

Discussing needed adaptations.

Photo courtesy of D. Juntunen.

○ Adapt the equipment to best suit the paddler and optimize the paddler's abilities.

○ Be conservative! There is no need to overoutfit the equipment. If you need only some additional support to the backband or seat to stabilize the lower back, then there is no need to build up lateral support. Build the necessary structure to maximize functional ability and adapt to compensate for decreased or lost function—nothing more, nothing less.

○ All adaptations should at first be temporary to be sure they meet the person's need. Use materials that can be easily adjusted and removed, such as duct tape and closed-cell foams that do not absorb water. Adaptations must be tested with the student on land before the first instructional session on water. If the outfitting does not feel comfortable, supportive, and stable to the student on land, then it will not work on water.

3. Keep it safe.

○ Ensure that the adaptation fits comfortably and the paddler can easily exit from the craft or release the paddle. For each paddler the potential risk factors need to be anticipated and minimized based on the craft, the type of paddling, adaptations, and the paddler's impairments.

○ *Never* bind the paddler to the watercraft or paddle. Do not use Velcro, belts, tape, or any products or techniques that adhere the paddler to equipment. The paddler must be able to freely and independently exit all adaptations and paddling devices in the event of a capsize. This is one of the most important guidelines to follow to ensure the paddler's safety.

○ All rescues need to be tried in a safe setting before using the adaptations on an open body of water. For seat adaptations, practice wet exits and rescues. For hand adaptations, practice releasing the paddle, first on land and then in a controlled environment on water.

○ Cover exposed nuts, bolts, and other items that could cause skin abrasions.

○ Always have the student wear a properly fitted PFD when adapting a watercraft because the outfitting needs to fit and function when the student is wearing a PFD on the water.

Once you have identified a paddler's specific needs, you can evaluate manufactured seat or paddle adaptations as potential longer-term solutions. Manufactured adaptations can be useful to get a paddler in a boat quickly, but they can be dangerous if you don't fully understand a paddler's impairments. They might also affect the paddler's ability to release equipment or exit the boat when capsizing. If manufactured seats or paddle adaptations are available, it is very tempting to skip the learning about the paddler's specific needs and provide more adaptation than is needed.

Building a temporary adaptation with foam and other material allows you and the paddler to learn exactly what level of support the paddler needs in the boat and where the equipment needs to be adapted. While developing a solution, the student becomes aware of the concerns and considerations that go into developing a particular adaptation and learns why it is important to release the paddle independently at any time or easily exit the boat when capsizing. With this awareness, when the paddler switches to a manufactured solution, she will be able to evaluate how that adaptation will affect comfort, performance, and safety.

Remember, this book can cover only the basics of canoe and kayak adaptations in a low-tech manner. It offers information that, combined with your own observations, listening skills, and creativity, will help you create adaptations for paddlers' unique needs. Successful adaptations may come quickly, or they can be time-consuming. Often you will need to engage in creative problem solving with the student with a disability. This time provides an excellent opportunity to become acquainted. The right adaptation can open up the world of paddling for that student—a result that is definitely worth the time!

Outfitting for Optimal Performance

Paddling is an aerobic and active sport in which participants decide what type of paddling best suits their interests. Whether they are recreational canoeists on local flatwater rivers or adventuresome whitewater kayakers looking for more challenge, the mechanics of the activity remain the same despite various levels of exertion and range of motion.

A variety of muscle groups in the feet, legs, torso, arms, wrists, hands, and head work together to rotate, stabilize, grip, lift, push, and pull. Designing and building an adaptation is about maximizing the ability, performance, and joy on the water for paddlers who have less control over their muscles and less mobility, strength, or body awareness in particular areas. Specific ideas and outfitting adaptations that best illustrate this concept are listed in chapter 8.

To create stability in any area of the body, use the same principle that applies to splinting an injury: Splint the area above and below the injured area to achieve stability. For example, an injury to the forearm requires splinting from the hand to the elbow. Using this principle, if the loss of function is in the abdominal region, the adaptation needs to extend from the lower area (pelvis) to the next area of stability or structure (the ribs). See figure 7.1. This strategy allows the trunk to be stabilized without relying on the abdominal muscles for support.

An understanding of the fundamentals of boat control is also important for boat outfitting. To maximize the efficiency of paddling strokes, paddlers need to be connected to the boat and supported in a strong athletic posture—an upright sitting position. Paddlers might perform the elements of a forward stroke correctly, but if they are not connected properly to the boat, they will pull themselves forward, sliding within the craft instead of gliding with it through the water.

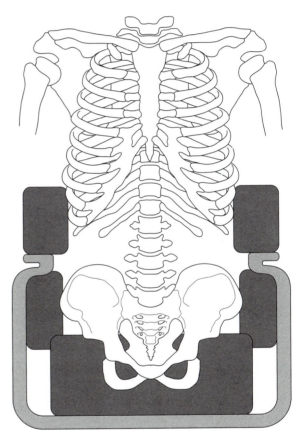

Figure 7.1
Additional support is needed to stabilize the ribs.

Five-Point Outfitting

A correctly fitted boat feels like an extension of the paddler's body. The paddler is able to control it by shifting weight, engaging and relaxing certain muscle groups, and pulling toward or pushing away from the paddle. To allow this type of control, a paddler needs at least five points of contact with the boat. In a kayak, the five

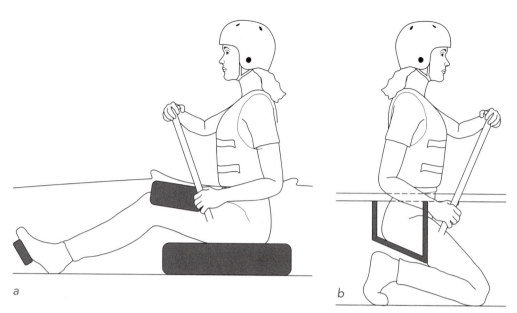

Figure 7.2
Five-point contact
in a (a) kayak and
a (b) canoe.

a   b

points are two feet, two thighs, and one buttock (see figure 7.2*a*). In a canoe, the five points are two feet, two knees, and one buttock, regardless of whether the canoeist is sitting or kneeling (see figure 7.2*b*).

Five-point outfitting refers to the number of contact points between the paddler's body and the boat that the outfitting tries to enhance. Having a firm surface to brace the feet against helps the paddler stay in the seat when performing a paddling stroke. Knees are bent and thighs or knees press against the boat sides to help control how much the boat is edged or leaned (the angle of the boat to the water). The fifth contact point, the buttock, is more like a complex contact area than a single contact point. It encompasses multiple contact points, where the weight of the paddler's upper body is distributed across the buttocks. The sides of the hips can connect with hip pads to prevent the paddler from sliding sideways in the boat, unintentionally shifting the weight and changing the boat lean. The lower back makes contact with a backband or other back support to incorporate and enhance a strong, upright sitting position.

If these aspects of outfitting are not addressed, the paddler will not be able to paddle efficiently and easily regardless of skill level. Paddlers who cannot maintain one or multiple contact points because of loss of function need alternative points of contact and alternative means of control.

Stable Seating

For every beginning paddler stability is high on the priority list. Capsizing and spending excessive time in the water while completing rescues is usually not an appealing thought for any beginner. The boat and adaptation must be designed for the desired type of water and allow the paddler to feel stable.

The seating position in the boat has a major impact on stability. If a paddler sits high in relation to the hull (shell of the boat), then the craft tips more easily. The feeling of stability improves as the paddler's center of gravity moves lower in the boat. Sometimes it is necessary to take out the seat that came with the kayak and build a lower seat. However, only remove the seat if doing so does not hinder the structural integrity of the boat. (See the discussion of seating systems on p. 72.) The paddler's weight should also be equally distributed between the right (starboard) and left (port) sides and centrally between the front (bow) and the back (stern). When the weight distribution is correct, the boat sits level in the water.

Ballast is useful when working with people who have had lower-extremity amputations or lower-body paralysis with atrophy of muscle mass. For example, if a paddler has an amputation on the right leg and no ballast is used to balance the boat, then the boat will tilt to the left and feel unstable. The paddler can hold the boat level with muscle power, but doing so will expend a lot of energy and make many paddling maneuvers difficult. Some ballast secured to the hull in the area of the amputated leg will help the boat stay level without that paddler effort and the boat handling difficulties. (See suggestions for ballast on p. 96.)

Without adaptations, paddlers with loss of function in their lower limbs usually have very limited or no ability to brace their bodies inside the boat. To get a sense of how difficult it is to paddle without that internal boat contact, try paddling with your legs crossed inside a canoe or kayak. Without the ability to brace against the boat, it is difficult to stay balanced on the seat while putting in a powerful stroke. In a kayak, a rigid foam bulkhead placed in front of the kayak's foot braces combined with two short foam rolls under the knees can help compensate. The first step to creating stable seating for a kayaker with a loss of lower limb function is to ensure solid non-entrapping contact for their feet by creating a bulkhead upon which their feet will be braced. The bulkhead—usually a rigid foam wall positioned directly in front of the paddler's feet—prevents the feet from slipping and potentially getting entrapped in the boat. In a canoe a foam footrest can fulfill a similar function. The knee rolls are simply two 6- to 7-inch-wide (15 to 18 cm) rolls of soft closed-cell foam, usually 8 inches (20 cm) long, that are duct taped to keep them tightly rolled. They are not attached to the boat and will float free in the event of a capsize. Knee rolls help position the paddler's knees under the thigh braces and out to the sides of the boat. The wider the base, the greater stability. (See figure 7.3 for kayak and figure 7.4 for canoe seating systems.)

A paddler who has difficulty supporting the upper body in an upright sitting position and feels unstable can benefit from a few basic seat adaptations.

- A change in the angle of the seat bottom (higher in the front, lower in the back) achieved by adding a foam wedge to the front portion of the seat base creates a position that slightly raises the thighs in the front and lowers the buttocks in the rear of a person's seating area. This higher-in-front seat-base configuration is referred as the seating angle or as the "dump" in the seat in wheelchair seating lingo. The term *dump* is not technically a medical term, but is a word used in the medical field to describe the seating angle or posterior tilt of the hips (see figure 7.3).

- Adjustments to the back support could include raising the back support or increasing the seat back's angle of recline to allow the paddler to sit with some backward lean.

- Foam wedges between the paddler's hips and the boat can provide lateral support for the paddler's waist and torso.

A custom-designed seating system is often the only option for paddlers with trunk, back, and leg impairments to get the support they need. In a kayak the challenge is to enable the kayaker to brace inside the boat and fit a seat with proper cushioning. Canoes have no built-in seat back or seat sides, and the challenge is to build a rigid seat back and some kind of seat support. Figures 7.3 and 7.4 show models of canoe and kayak seating systems that have been used to customize seats in ACA Adaptive Paddling Workshops, in recreational programs, and on extended trips.

Kayak Seating System

The sequence of seating area adaptation development starts at the feet and works up the body. In a kayak, this begins with the installation of a bulkhead to support the lowest extremity and prevent entrapment. Once the bulkhead has been addressed, the legs and hips and torso are addressed in that order, to the extent required by the paddlers needs. The adaptation must include padding as necessary for skin protection. See figure 7.3.

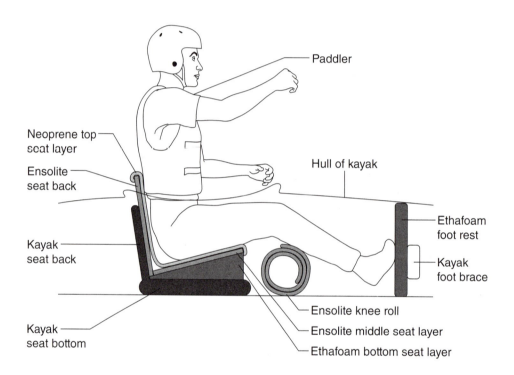

Figure 7.3
The kayak seating
system.

Elements

- *Bulkhead:* A properly fitted bulkhead keeps the paddler from slipping/sliding forward in the seat, and in the case of a capsize, getting entrapped deep in the boat or with their feet behind foot pegs.

- *Seat back:* Strong back support tilted slightly backward to help paddlers with limited trunk stability to stay upright and not fall forward.

- *High lateral support (not pictured):* Stops paddler from falling sideways.

- *Seat:* Multiple cushioning layers create a seating angle/dump in the seat to keep the paddler from sliding forward. The original seating system needs to be removed when many layers are needed to create the right shape for the seat. Otherwise, the paddler will sit too high and be unstable.

- *Knee rolls:* Keep the knees and legs to the sides of the boat and help with balance, if a paddler has no control over lower limbs.

- *Layering system:* Use the layers depending on the needs of the paddler.

Canoe Seating System

The sequence of seating area adaptation development starts at the feet and works toward the head. In a canoe, this begins with the recognition that a nonslip surface or footrest and under thigh structure will be needed to support the lowest extremity, with hips and torso addressed in that order, and to the extent required by the paddlers needs. The adaptation must include padding as necessary for skin protection. See figure 7.4.

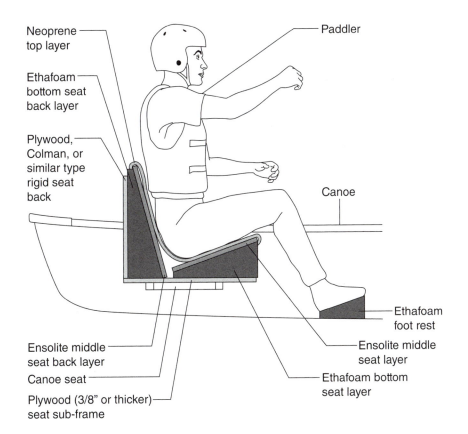

Neoprene top layer
Ethafoam bottom seat back layer
Plywood, Colman, or similar type rigid seat back
Paddler
Canoe
Ethafoam foot rest
Ensolite middle seat back layer
Canoe seat
Plywood (3/8" or thicker) seat sub-frame
Ensolite middle seat layer
Ethafoam bottom seat layer

Figure 7.4
The canoe seating system.

Elements

- *Seat back:* Create back support with plywood and foam.
- *Seat:* Enlarge seat area to fit the adaptation and reinforce it with plywood.
- *Seat and seat back:* Form a seating angle/dump to support the paddler in the seat.
- *Footrest:* Sometimes a nonskid material placed under the paddler's feet is enough. A piece of Ethafoam may be necessary to create a footrest so the paddler's feet and legs are not dangling and to prevent the paddler from slipping/sliding forward in the seat.
- *Layering system:* Use the layers depending on the needs of the paddler.

Use these models as a starting point to create your own seating adaptations. Leverage elements of these seating systems and combine them with existing outfitting that already serves the purpose. Chapter 8 has more examples of how elements of these systems are used in adaptations or combined with new ideas. There are no limits to your creativity as long as you remember the following:

- Listen to paddlers with disabilities and design for their needs.
- Keep it simple.
- Keep it safe.

Mobility and Safety

Essential support and stability needs to be balanced with *mobility*. For a paddler who needs a lot of support (e.g., high lateral support in the torso area), mobility can be an issue. The adaptation must allow the paddler to move many different body parts while stroking and even support these movements. Otherwise, it decreases stroke efficiency and effectiveness and undermines overall paddling comfort. An adaptation that limits mobility can also cause safety problems, such as preventing a paddler from safely exiting a craft. The paddler should have freedom to move the arms, shoulders, and torso without compromising stability and safety.

One consideration that dominates all other adaptation decisions is *safety*. Paddlers have to know that they can rely on an adaptation when they need it, and they have to be confident that at any time they can safely exit the craft and release the paddle without the help of another person. The bulkhead in front of the paddler's feet ensures that no limb can slip behind a foot brace and get trapped. Ethafoam can fill the space under the cockpit rim or combing to minimize the risk of toes getting caught. The outfitting must be securely attached either to the boat or the paddle, not the paddler. It is essential to test adaptations and practice wet exits, paddle releases, and rescues before venturing out on a trip. Regular practice gives confidence that equipment and adaptation are safe and reliable and that the process of releasing and wet exiting is easy and fast.

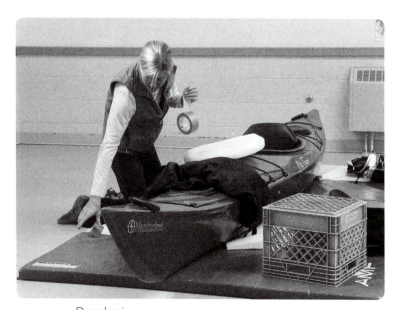

Developing adaptations.
Photo courtesy of D. Juntunen.

Skin Protection

The largest body organ is the skin, which is greatly affected by pressure, abrasion, and water conditions related to paddling. The skin is a delicate organ that can take some serious abuse. For people with impairments that do not allow them to feel their skin, however, skin problems can cause serious, even life-threatening, issues if not addressed. When a person loses skin sensation, which commonly occurs with a spinal cord injury, the skin can begin to break down in a matter of minutes if not properly protected. Equipment adaptations for a paddler who has skin sensitivity must be developed with skin protection as a primary concern. (See Skin: The Body's Biggest Organ System in appendix D for additional information.)

Carefully check the inside of the canoe or kayak for rough surfaces and sharp edges, and then remove or pad those areas. Cover exposed nuts, bolts, and other items that could cause skin abrasions. Pipe insulation works well to cover the metal rails that are holding foot pegs and foot braces in place. The adaptation itself needs to be padded and covered with nonabrasive types of foam. A layering system is useful to combine comfort with adequate support (see p. 76 in this chapter).

A good seat adaptation fits the paddler snugly, but it does not prevent the paddler from lifting up from the seat frequently to do a pressure release, allowing blood flow to the seat and lower extremities. The person can add further protection by wearing long pants and water socks or booties. Neoprene or other seamless gloves work well for hand protection, but avoid cycling gloves. The straps and cloth or leather on cycling gloves can make it difficult to exit the adaptation.

Wheelchair Seat Cushions and Paddling

If you are paddling with someone who uses medical items in daily life, remember that such items are designed for land-based activities and should not be used as part of a boat's outfitting or adaptation. A fairly frequent request from paddlers who use wheelchairs is to use their removable wheelchair seat cushions as part of a boat's seating adaptation. If the person has lower-limb paralysis, the wheelchair seat cushion is specially designed to provide positioning as well as deep cushioning for skin protection. However, most of these expensive wheelchair cushions are not designed for use out of the wheelchair or in water environments.

The gel cushions that are the primary form of cushioning in a wheelchair should not be used in a paddling adaptation for a variety of reasons. Paddling requires a different seated position than propelling a wheelchair does. Paddling mechanics promote greater torso rotation than the mechanics of propelling a wheelchair, which is more of a linear motion. Gel cushions allow for movement forward and back as well as side to side, which creates an unstable base for the paddler. These cushions are usually 3 to 4 inches (8 to 11 cm) thick, raising the center of gravity on water and further undermining stability. They will also sink to the bottom of the waterway in the event of a capsize.

Gel cushions manufactured for paddling, such as the Yakpad, can be secured to boat seats. This type of cushion in approximately 1/4-inch (0.6 cm) thick and is designed to provide comfort on a manufactured seat of plastic or fiberglass. This type of cushion is an alternative for a paddler looking for a low-profile cushion to provide comfort. However, it is not recommended for use by a paddler who has decreased circulation or sensation because it will not provide the amount of support or cushion needed to protect the tissue exposed to the gel seat.

Some wheelchair seating cushions designed with individual independent air cells are okay to get wet; however, they use the wheelchair's framework to provide the needed structure for proper support. Further, when used as part of the boat's seating adaptation, the individual air cells result in increased seating instability. The paddler moves slightly forward and back as well as side to side on the air cells while the boat moves across the water, and the water itself is also moving—an unstable combination.

Rather than using the person's wheelchair cushion, use multilayer closed-cell foam to create a stable seat that also provides the necessary cushioning properties and seating position. Meanwhile, the paddler's wheelchair cushion remains dry and secure with the wheelchair, ready for the paddler's return from paddling. Work with the paddler to develop confidence in the cushioning properties of closed-cell foams. Then, together determine the types and degree of layering that will be needed for a seating system.

When designing the outfitting or adaptation, use the medical equipment as a guide. Try to understand why the seat was designed in a certain way and model your alternative seat with these considerations in mind. The paddler's own wheelchair cushion can be a useful guide concerning the placement of various depths of the foam as well as the shaping and angles of the seat to best meet the needs of that paddler. You can build a similar skin-protective and supportive seat with material appropriate for use in the water.

The Layering System

Seat adaptation is a system of layering determined by the individual paddler's needs, the type of craft, and the paddling environment. Once you understand the principles of the layering system, you will be ready to customize the seating to meet the needs of each paddler. If you adhere to the principle of keeping it simple, you don't need to invest in a large bundle of supplies. A basic kit of duct tape, a variety of pieces of closed-cell foam, and some household tools is all you need to start exploring adaptations. Pack the basic tool kit items into a big plastic box for transport to the pool or shoreline, and you are ready to begin. See table 7.2 on page 80.

Foam is the essential building block of any adaptation. The most commonly used materials are various types of closed-cell foam, which have excellent characteristics for use in water. They don't soak up water or deteriorate when wet; they also float,

Environmental Effects on Adaptive Equipment and Adhesives

Heat

- Cements tend to dry faster in warm temperatures.
- Glues and adhesives tend to deteriorate in warm weather.
- The rubber in hand adaptations tends to loosen in warm weather.
- Foams and plastics that are dark in color generate a high level of heat, which has a negative effect on the adaptive adhesives and can injure and burn the participant's skin.

Cold

- Cold can make it very difficult to apply adhesives.
- Cements take longer to dry in cold weather.
- Tape becomes less pliable in cold weather.
- Foams become more rigid and may lose some cushioning properties in cold weather.

Water

- Wet conditions can make it impossible to apply adhesives.
- Cements will not bond to wet surfaces.
- Tapes will not bond to wet surfaces.
- Foam will try to float if submerged.

which adds additional buoyancy. Environmental conditions can affect foam, so read the additional tips in the sidebar Environmental Effects on Adaptive Equipment and Adhesives on page 76 before you begin to build adaptations.

To understand foam characteristics and the role of foam in building an adaptation, it helps to think of a seating adaptation as a system of layers:

- Layer 1 is farthest from the skin and provides structural support.
- Layer 2 gives the adaptation contours, seating angles, and provides some padding.
- Layer 3 is next to the skin and provides cushioning.
- Layer 4 is mainly for beautification.

The only truly optional layer is the beautification layer. If the adaptation has been constructed carefully and all duct tape is smooth and even in length, there will be minimal need for top dressing the adaptation to make it more attractive. Although an added layer for beautification purposes only may be tempting, be sure that layer is also appropriate for the paddler's final fit within the boat.

Layer 1: Structure and Support

Ethafoam is a type of foam that can be used farthest from the skin to build structure and support. Ethafoam is a medium-weight, fairly rigid foam that is good for light structural use. It can be cut and carved fairly easily with hand saws, SureFoam, or a bread knife. It can be used in a kayak for a bulkhead that will serve as a foot brace, for an extra-high back, and for lateral torso support. In a canoe you can build additional support under the seat for larger people. This foam has a rough texture, so it should never be used in direct contact with skin. You can buy it from some kayak and canoe mail order companies and from aircraft supply companies. Also, many boatbuilders have this type of foam. The foam is relatively inexpensive and usually sold in planks. Planks that are 2 to 3 inches (5 to 8 cm) thick are most useful. It is not recommended to use Styrofoam because it does not meet the foam requirements and because it can break apart in the environment.

Layer 2: Contour and Cushion

Minicell foam is used in the second layer; it has good flexibility and padding characteristics. It helps contour, refine the angles, and cushion the rougher, more rigid Ethafoam under it. Minicell foam carves quite well with a matte knife, SureFoam, or keyhole saw, and it can be used as a structural component. These characteristics make Minicell especially valuable when creating a socket for a paddler with a leg amputation or when shaping thigh braces. It is the most common after-market material used in boat outfitting and can be found at any professional paddling shop.

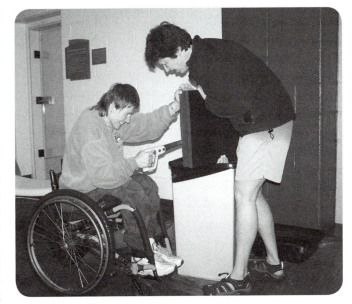

Cutting foam for the adaptation.

Photo courtesy of R. Mravetz.

Layer 3: Next to the Skin

The third layer is created from Ensolite. Approximately 3/4 to 1 inch (2 to 2.5 cm) thick, this foam gives the most cushion without losing structure and can be used as a next-to-the-skin layer. Sold in sheets, Ensolite can be easily cut with scissors or a matte knife, but it cannot be easily carved and shaped. The best sources are plastic and rubber supply manufacturers or local upholstery shops. Ensolite varies in density and therefore in its ability to rebound quickly when compressed—qualities that, along with thickness, are crucial to the cushioning effect needed for skin protection. This rebound effect can be checked by pinching the foam tightly between your thumb and index finger for five to six seconds and then letting go. The foam should very quickly rebound to its original shape and thickness. This is also referred to as foam memory.

For seating adaptation development to maximize skin protection, use 1-inch-thick (2.5 cm) Ensolite, which you have tested to ensure that it has the necessary quick rebound properties. The foam should have the same depth throughout (no imperfections, dimples, or ridges) and be smooth on both sides. The Ensolite found at camping supply stores is usually of a lesser quality, and it should only be used for adaptations that don't bear weight, such as knee rolls, or for adding flotation to equipment.

Layer 4: Finishing Touches

Neoprene can be used as a finishing layer to provide a clean finish, especially on adaptations with a longer life expectancy. Strive to make adaptations aesthetically pleasing. No one wants to paddle an ugly boat. Neoprene also provides greater traction than Ensolite when wet and helps prevent paddlers from slipping in their seats. It can pad rough areas on boats and be used for paddle adaptations. Available from paddlers' supply stores and diving shops, it comes in sheets ranging in thickness from 1/8 to 1/4 inch (0.3 to 0.6 cm) for useful finishing layers. Special care should be taken with participants with latex sensitivities or allergies; most neoprene has a high latex component. Alternative resources are fleece materials or lamb's wool.

Not every seating adaptation will require the use of each of the four layers. However, if a layer is left out of an adaptation, usually another piece of equipment is taking its place. For example, if the necessary structural support already exists in the boat, only contouring and padding next to the skin and to provide cushioning might be needed. At other times, for example, when a seat back has to be rebuilt, the key to the adaptation is structural support. Padding on the seat back and on lateral supports can be minimal because the paddler's life jacket will provide padding in those locations. However, it is essential to add appropriate cushioning layers of soft closed-cell foam for skin protection wherever skin that has reduced sensation or has been injured will be touching any surface of the boat. The extra cushioning layer can sometimes be skipped in an area that bears no weight, such as the foot brace or bulkhead, because the paddler will be wearing foot protection. However, if the paddler has had an injury or has skin sensitivity in areas that will be touching the foot brace or bulkhead, then the cushioning layer must also be used there.

Basic Tool Kit

Use the measurements and quantities in table 7.1 as a guide for how much and what types of foam you should have available to build a complete custom seat. One foam kit combined with a large roll of duct tape usually provides enough material to outfit a paddler. See table 7.2 for additional supplies to create the custom seats.

Table 7.1   Quantity and Types of Foams Needed for Adaptations

CANOE KIT		
Measurement	Material	Quantity
1/2-3 1/2 in. (1.3-8.9 cm) thick × 16 in. (41 cm) L × 16 in. (41 cm) W	Minicell wedges	2
1/2-3 1/2 in. (1.3-8.9 cm) thick × 16 in. (41 cm) L × 8 in. (20 cm) W	Minicell wedges	4
18 in. (46 cm) W × 42 in. (107 cm) L × 1 in. (2.5 cm) thick	Ensolite plank	1
18 in. (46 cm) W × 24 in. (61 cm) L × 2 in. (5 cm) thick	Ethafoam plank	1
KAYAK KIT		
1/2-3 1/2 in. (1.3-8.9 cm) thick × 16 in. (41 cm) L × 16 in. (41 cm) W	Minicell wedges	2
1/2-3 1/2 in. thick × 16 (41 cm) L × 8 in. (20 cm) W	Minicell wedges	4
18 in. (46 cm) W × 42 in. (107 cm) L × 1 in. (2.5 cm) thick	Ensolite plank	1
18 in. (46 cm) W × 24 in. (61 cm) L × 2 in. (5 cm) thick	Ethafoam plank	1

Table 7.2 A Basic Tool Kit for Creating Custom Seats

Tool or material	Use
Small crosscut saw or drywall saw	Cut Ethafoam or Minicell foams.
Hole saw	Cut in tight areas or make curved cuts.
Phillips head screwdriver, blade screwdriver, and a few wrenches from a bicycle tool kit	Take out or adjust existing kayak seats and thigh braces.
Metal ruler	Measure foam before cutting and draw straight lines.
Matte knife or razor knife	Cut foam.
Scissors	Cut tape and Ensolite.
Brad knife	Cut and carve Minicell, cut Ethafoam, and also make intricate cuts.
Contact cement or adhesive sprays (such as Clearco 444)	Form a strong bond between foams and other similar or dissimilar materials. Make sure the contact cement or spray retains a strong bond in water and does not contain solvents that dissolve foams. Use in well-ventilated area.
Small brushes	Apply contact cement.
Medium-thick picture wire or other wire	Create templates (e.g., to form the shape and size of a foam bulkhead).
Duct tape	Temporarily attach an adaptation before attaching it more permanently to the boat. Apply the tape as smoothly as possible. Even small wrinkles and folds can contribute to skin abrasion for a paddler who has lost skin sensation.
Measuring tape	Measure twice, cut once!
1 liter plastic bottle (2)	Fill with water or wet sand and use as ballast to balance the boat in the event of a weight discrepancy in lower extremities.
Permanent marker	Mark cutting area on foam.
Zip ties	Primarily to secure hand adaptations to the paddle.
Mountain bike inner tube	For hand adaptations.
Wooden board	Use as work surface.

Building a Bulkhead

Paddlers who have impairments in their lower extremities should use a bulkhead while paddling any boat with a cockpit. The bulkhead protects the paddler from entrapment and provides a base of support. Located in the bow of the boat, it is a flat surface erected in front of the paddler's feet. See the How to Build a Bulkhead sidebar on this page.

How to Build a Bulkhead

To build a bulkhead, use a sheet of Ethafoam that is the width and height of the boat in the location where it will be secured. The following steps will guide you through the process:

1. Measure the length of the participant's lower extremity from the hip to the most distal part of the extremity.
2. Measure from the seat to the bow using the measurement from step 1 (after all seat modifications have been completed). This point in the bow will be the bulkhead's location.
3. Use a piece of wire, such as picture wire, to form a mold around the boat's exterior at the measured point.
4. Take the molded wire and draw the pattern on the Ethafoam.
5. Use a crosscut saw to cut the Ethafoam.
6. Remove thigh braces if doing so does not compromise the boat's structural integrity.
7. Remove all foot braces or slide them beyond the bulkhead.
8. Make notches in the Ethafoam if the foot braces attach to rails.
9. Place the cut Ethafoam bulkhead in the boat. It should fit tightly into place.
10. Use a piece of SureFoam if needed to modify the bulkhead to fit securely.
11. Have the paddler transfer into the boat to check the bulkhead's location.
12. The paddler must be in a position from which she can wet exit independently by bringing her lower extremities into the boat's midline.
13. If a paddler is unable to complete step 12, trim off a small portion of the bulkhead's outer edge on all sides using SureFoam, and repeat steps 11 and 12.
14. If the watercraft has a beam down the centerline, you must make two separate bulkheads for each side.
15. If the paddler's lower extremities have different lengths (such as in the case of an amputation), you can make two separate bulkheads if another contact point will enhance the paddler's ability. Ensure there are no voids between the two bulkheads.

Adaptations Based on Functional Impairments

This chapter provides examples of useful adaptations that have worked for various paddlers and ideas to inspire new adaptations based on your own observations, listening skills, and creativity. What keeps the task interesting, challenging, and fun is that each paddler requires a unique solution for his or her outfitting. There are no cookie-cutter templates to follow because each paddler is unique in body shape, abilities, and interests. Two paddlers might have a similar functional impairment, but they may require completely different adaptations based on the extent of their function, their experience, and differences in flexibility and strength.

Use the following examples as guidance to create an initial adaptation. Observe how the adaptation works on dry land and calm water in controlled conditions and adjust it as needed. Remember: The paddler needs to be able to independently exit the craft and release the paddle so safety isn't compromised. Once you have identified the right level and type of adaptations, you can refine the design for long-term use and beautify it.

See chapter 6 for paddling and teaching suggestions based on loss of function. Chapters 6 and 8 are designed as cross-referenced tools.

UPPER LIMB (ARM AND HAND)

Commonly Related Conditions

arthritis, cerebral palsy, hemiplegia, quadriplegia, multiple sclerosis

Possible Implications for Paddling: Teaching Suggestions and Adaptations

Weakness in forearm or hand and unable to grasp paddle firmly

For a paddler who has difficulty holding a paddle firmly, try a lightweight, unfeathered, straight-shaft paddle. If the paddler still has difficulty, an adaptation for just the weaker hand may be enough to provide sufficient paddle control. If not, adapt for both hands, adding to the adaptation's complexity as necessary.

At first a hand adaptation may feel tight enough; however, as the person begins to paddle, he may find his hands slipping out of the adaptation after every few strokes. In that case, first give some pointers based on your observation of the paddler's technique before rushing to change the adaptation.

Examples of technique tips to try first:

- Encourage the paddler to push with one hand while pulling with the other hand. To conserve energy, the paddler can relax the hand that is pushing.

- Sea kayakers or lake paddlers may want to use more of a touring stroke than a power forward stroke. During the touring stroke, the paddle shaft is held in a more relaxed, lower position relative to the water surface, and the paddle blade moves farther from the kayak very naturally. The paddle moves less forcefully through the water, so the shoulders, arms, and hands can conserve energy.

- Ensure that the paddler slices up with the paddle blade's edge coming out of the water cleanly at the stroke's end rather than lifting the flat face of paddle blade up from the water and in doing so lifting the water with it. Rotating the torso, if possible, not only provides additional power for the stroke, but also makes the slicing and lifting motion more natural.

Developing a paddle grip adaptation.

Photo courtesy of Northeast Passage-NH.

Oversized paddle grip (canoe or kayak)

An oversized grip helps paddlers who have difficulty fully closing their hands to hold the paddle more comfortably (see figure 8.1). This grip adaptation requires only two simple items: duct tape and pipe insulation foam. Wrap the paddle shaft and grip with a 6-inch (15 cm) length of foam where the hand will be gripping the paddle shaft; then tape the foam in place. You can adjust the size by trimming the foam or wrapping the tape tighter around the area. Apply the tape carefully to avoid folds and creases that can easily create blisters or wounds from abrasion.

Figure 8.1 Oversized paddle grip.

Bicycle style paddle grips

Bicycle style paddle grips can be cut, placed on the paddle, and secured with tape (see figure 8.2). Grips with finger grooves help the paddler keep her hand placement on the shaft as she grasps the paddle.

Figure 8.2 Bicycle style paddle grip.

Inner-tube paddle grip adaptation on a paddle shaft (canoe or kayak)

The inner-tube paddle grip is an easy and inexpensive adaptation that can compensate for a lack of grip strength (see figure 8.3). It requires only pieces of a used mountain bike inner tube and cable or zip ties. If a person also needs the oversized grip, build the oversized grip first.

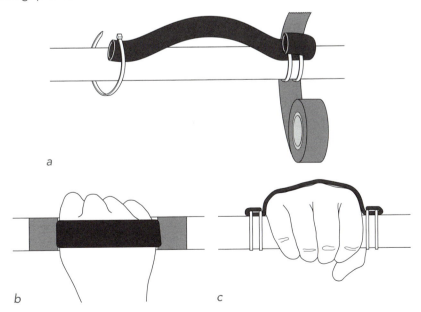

Figure 8.3 Mountain bike inner-tube paddle grip: (a) construction, (b) top view, and (c) front view.

For the inner-tube paddle grip, cut a piece of used mountain bike inner tube about 10 inches (25 cm) long. Mark the paddler's hand position on the paddle shaft with a line on both sides of the hand. Place one inner-tube strip along the shaft over the hand lines. On the hand line closest to the middle of the paddle, put a zip tie around the paddle and pull it tight. Put another zip tie around the paddle and inner tube at the other hand line. Tighten this one only a little so that it barely holds the inner tube to the paddle. If a paddler needs this grip support for both hands, repeat this process for the other hand.

Ask the paddler to put his hands through the inner tube section. Pull the end of the inner tube through the loose zip tie until the inner tube is just tight enough to hold the paddle to the hand. If the paddler is planning to wear gloves on the water, the adaptation needs to be fitted with the gloves on. Make sure the paddler can pull his hand out of the adaptation and off the paddle without needing to use the other hand.

After checking that the person can release the paddle safely, tighten the loose zip tie all the way. To hold the inner tube in place, you may have to use two zip ties on each end of the inner tube.

Caution: Rotate all zip-tie heads away from the paddler's hands, cut the ends of the zip ties, and fold excess tubing over the zip tie heads, securing and covering the ends with duct tape. After completing the adaptation, recheck that the paddler can release the paddle independently.

When the paddler's hands or the paddle adaptations get wet, the hand may slip out of the adaptation, so the adaptation will need to be tightened again. Open the zip tie and tighten it, add a zip tie closer to the hand, or cut off the existing tie and replace it with a tighter zip tie.

Inner-tube paddle grip adaptation (canoe only)

You can create an adjustable paddle adaptation for the T-grip of a canoe paddle with a piece of used mountain bike inner tube, about 3 to 4 inches (8 to 10 cm) of clear tube (or PVC pipe), and zip ties. The clear tube (1 inch, or 2.5 cm, in diameter) is usually used for refrigeration drainpipes. You can also cut a piece of an old garden hose to use in place of the clear tube.

Using a 12-inch-long (30 cm) piece of used mountain bike inner tube, make a loop about 3 inches (8 cm) in diameter and place it on top of the T-grip (see figure 8.4). One end of the inner tube should overlap the rest of the tube by almost 3 inches (8 cm). Hold the overlapping parts of the inner tube on top of the T-grip, and place the clear tube over the overlapped inner tube ends. One end of the inner tube should stick out from under the clear tube at the end of the paddle grip. By pulling on this end, you can tighten the loop.

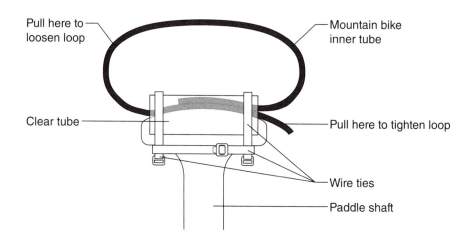

Figure 8.4
Inner-tube paddle grip adaptation for a T-grip canoe paddle.

Put two zip ties around the clear tube near each end and tighten them loosely. Have the paddler put a hand through the loop. The back of the hand just past the knuckles should be covered by the inner tube. The adaptation should help the paddler maintain a grip on the paddle, but it should *not* tie the hand to the paddle. The person must be able to release the paddle when needed. If the adaptation is too loose, pull the loose end of the inner tube. If it is too tight, pull on the inner tube at the other end of the clear tube.

On some T-grips, the zip ties tend to slip off the ends of the grip. You can create a little harness with two additional zip ties. Place one zip tie across the front of the paddle through the initial two zip ties and tighten it. Do the same in the back with one more zip tie Cut the ends of the zip ties and rotate them away from the hand and cover them with duct tape.

ABS plastic paddle grip adaptations (canoe or kayak)

If you have the resources, you can create more substantial paddle grip adaptations of ABS plastic. These paddle grip adaptations are also available commercially.

The paddle shaft grip supports the hand on the shaft of a canoe or kayak paddle (see figure 8.5). Once created, it can be reused many times and easily fitted to various paddles and paddlers. The adaptation consists of a piece of ABS plastic, Velcro straps, hose clamp or zip ties, and some soft closed-cell foam or neoprene. A variation is designed for a canoe paddle's T-grip (see figure 8.6).

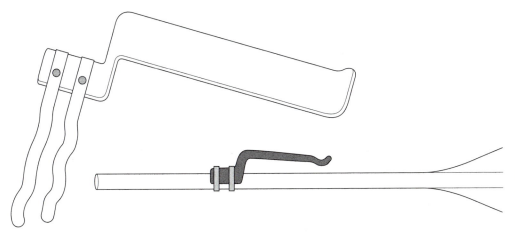

Figure 8.5
ABS paddle shaft grip adaptations (canoe or kayak).

For the paddle shaft grip, the end of the ABS plastic is shaped to snap on a paddle shaft and is strapped on tightly with Velcro or a zip tie, while the other end extends in an arc across the back of the paddler's hand on the paddle shaft. For the T-grip, the ABS plastic extends over the hand on the top of the T-grip with the opening to one end of the top of the T-bar so the paddler can slide her hand out of the adaptation. The adaptation attaches to the paddle shaft below the top T-bar (see figure 8.6). Depending on the dimension of the paddle shaft, soft foam or neoprene can be used as padding between the plastic and the hand, and can also be used to create an oversized grip across the T-bar.

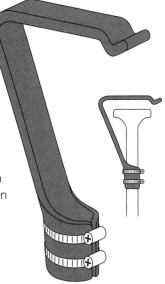

Figure 8.6
ABS canoe paddle T-grip adaptation.

Materials to create an ABS plastic paddle grip:

- ABS plastic sheet approximately 1 1/2 inches (4 cm) wide and 12 inches (30 cm) long
- Two to four rivets
- Self-adhering Velcro strap about 10 inches (25 cm) long
- 2-inch (5 cm) section of a used mountain bike inner tube
- 2-inch × 6-inch (5 × 15 cm) piece of Ensolite foam
- Duct tape
- Tools: propane torch, two pairs of pliers, rivet gun, hand drill, and drill bits

Use a band saw or jigsaw to cut the plastic into 1 1/2-inch (4 cm) by 12-inch (30 cm) strips; then sand down all the corners and sharp edges. To create the shape of the hand adaptation, heat and shape each bend separately. To protect yourself, make sure to wear thick gloves and work in a well-ventilated area. The fumes from the plastic are unhealthy and flammable. Slowly heat the ABS plastic at one end until pliable. Once it is pliable, bend the plastic to the desired shape, hold it about 60 seconds in this new shape, and let it cool. Execute only one bend per heating to ensure proper positioning. The material loses integrity if it is reheated and becomes more likely to break. Work from the open end of the adaptation to the end that attaches to the paddle.

The last tricky heating-and-shaping step creates the last bend in the adaptation and shapes the end around the paddle, so you can easily snap it to the paddle later. Once the plastic is shaped, check to see if you need to sand down some edges or sharp corners. Then drill two holes in the portion that will attach to the paddle shaft. Attach the Velcro and inner-tube piece to this portion with rivets. The Velcro goes on the outside to strap the adaptation to the paddle. The inner tube goes on the inside to make the adaptation sit more securely on the paddle shaft (see figure 8.5 on p. 87). You should now be able to Velcro the adaptation to the paddle. To adjust the fit to the size of the paddlers hand, tape Ensolite foam to the underside of the plastic grip where it passes over the paddler's hand. Make sure the paddler can both control the paddle and release it quickly and independently when needed.

Paddle grip adaptations based on the above designs are commercially available from Chosen Valley Creating Ability (www.creatingability.com).

Possible Implications for Paddling: Teaching Suggestions and Adaptations

Inability to grasp paddle

As explained in chapter 6 (see p. 47), people should not use prostheses when paddling unless they are designed for water use and allow paddlers to independently and quickly release the paddle from the prosthesis. The adaptations listed in this section are possible alternatives.

Built-up paddle grip or shaft

Whether canoeing or kayaking, the paddler may be able to hold a paddle with either the grip or paddle shaft located under the residual limb. Be sure to properly build up the paddle portion held under the residual limb with closed-cell foam for an easier grip and more comfort. The best foam to use in this situation is Ensolite or a soft, closed-cell type that will not irritate the paddler's skin.

A little adjustment.
Photo courtesy of Northeast Passage-NH.

Kickboard paddle

A paddler with one arm may use a wooden kickboard often used by swimmers or a similarly sized smooth, lightweight piece of wood (12 to 18 inches, or 30 to 46 cm) with a handhold cut-out. However, paddling with this adaptation is fatiguing (see figure 8.7).

Single arm adapted paddle

In this adaptation, a paddle blade and part of the shaft is combined with a crutchlike upper portion (see figure 8.8).

Figure 8.7
Kickboard paddle.

Figure 8.8
Adapted paddle.

Terminal device

TRS Inc. makes a terminal device called the Hammerhead, which mounts to a waterproof prosthesis and is designed for kayaking and canoeing (see figure 8.9). A strap from the Hammerhead wraps around the paddle and is secured over a large knob on the device. The connection with the paddle is strong and flexible. When paddling with a small shaft, the Hammerhead sometimes slips along the paddle shaft. You can prevent slippage by wrapping and taping some foam on the paddle shaft on both sides of the Hammerhead.

The Hammerhead features a grip at the end of the strap that can be pulled or pushed to release the paddle. A person using this device needs to have the strength and flexibility as well as adequate practice to release the paddle independently at any time. A concern are situations in which the paddle gets entangled and pulled behind the paddler's back or over the head with the Hammerhead's release mechanism out of reach. When this adaptation is used, emphasize clean paddle strokes when teaching to avoid torque on the socket.

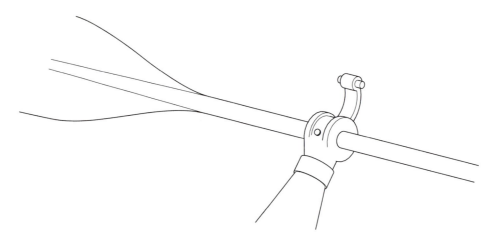

Figure 8.9
Terminal device.

Commonly Related Conditions

cerebral palsy, paraplegia, quadriplegia (affecting trunk balance)

Possible Implications for Paddling: Teaching Suggestions and Adaptations

Limited neck or torso rotation

Bicycle rearview mirror
A small rearview mirror can be mounted on the boat or the paddler's hat for a wider view.

Difficulty sitting unsupported; balance affected

Basic principles for adaptations that provide seat support and stability are described in the section Stable Seating on page 70 in chapter 7.

High seat back for large paddlers (kayak)
For large paddlers who need a lot of backward lean in their upper bodies to remain stable in a seat, use a variation of the kayak seating system described in the Stable Seating section on page 70 in chapter 7. The seat back's structural support is provided by a wedge of Ethafoam covered with a Minicell layer. The Ethafoam is backed by another Ethafoam wedge that is built up from the cockpit rim behind the seat. In an open recreational kayak the back support needs to be built up from the kayak floor to the seat back (see Kayak Seating System, figure 7.3 on p. 72 for kayaks and see Canoe Seating System, figure 7.4 on p. 73 for canoes, both in chapter 7).

C-bend wrap (kayak)
For large paddlers who have difficulty sitting upright, a C-bend wrap is another variation of a kayak seating system that provides not only back but also lateral support. Take a piece of Ethafoam about 18 inches (46 cm) wide, 48 inches (122 cm) long, and 2 inches (5 cm) thick and wrap it around the back and sides of the seating area in the shape of the letter C (see figure 8.10). Ask the paddler to transfer into the kayak to try the fit of the seat. The Ethafoam on each side of the paddler needs to be cut low enough to allow arm movement when paddling but still remain high enough to provide necessary lateral support. Use a fine-point marker to mark the foam where it should be cut. The Ethafoam will curve from the high seat back downward to the sides that form the lower lateral support. Once you have cut and contoured the Ethafoam to the paddler's needs, secure the seat base and back with duct tape. Cushion the Ethafoam that provides lateral support as needed to protect the paddler's skin.

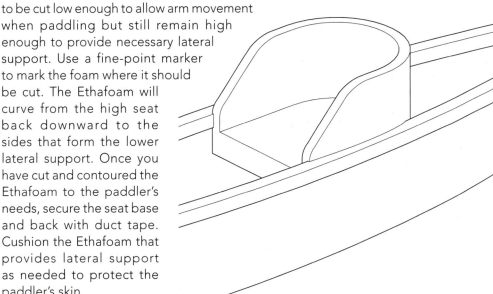

Figure 8.10
C-bend wrap seating for a kayak.

Wedges for lateral support (kayak)

You can use Minicell foam wedges to create lateral support for the paddler's upper body. Prepare multiple wedges about 3 1/2 inches (9 cm) thick at one end and narrowing down to 1/2 inch (1.3 cm) thick at the other end, 16 inches (41 cm) long, and 8 inches (20 cm) wide (see figure 8.11). With the paddler seated in the kayak seat, slide the Minicell wedges into the cockpit at the hips. Carve the wedges as needed so that they support the paddler, but don't limit mobility. Make sure that the paddler can make a quick and clean exit of the kayak in the event of a capsize. Secure the wedges with duct tape.

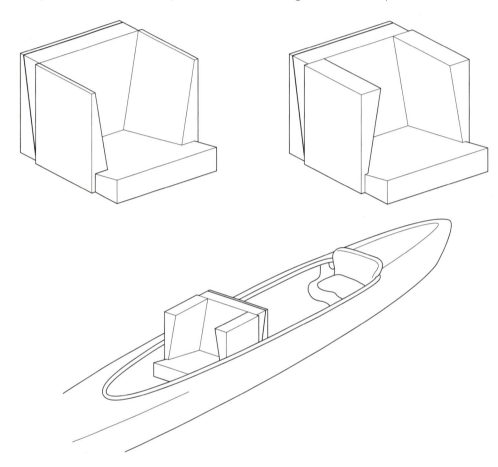

Figure 8.11
Wedges for lateral
support.

Custom canoe seating systems

Unlike kayaks, canoes do not have built-in seat backs and seat sides. For a paddler who has difficulty sitting unsupported, you will have to build a rigid seat back and some kind of lateral or side support. Check the guidelines for a canoe seating system on page 73 in chapter 7.

Commercial canoe seat backs

Several canoe manufacturers provide seat backs for canoe seats. Probably the most convenient seat back styles attach to the existing seat through hooks or straps (see figure 8.12). If there is any doubt about the seat back's strength, a piece of line can be used like a backband to support it. Each end of the line is secured to the front portion of the seat in a manner that does not impede a quick exit from the canoe in the event of a capsize. Any side panels or structure of the seat can serve as a frame to which foam wedges can be attached as side supports.

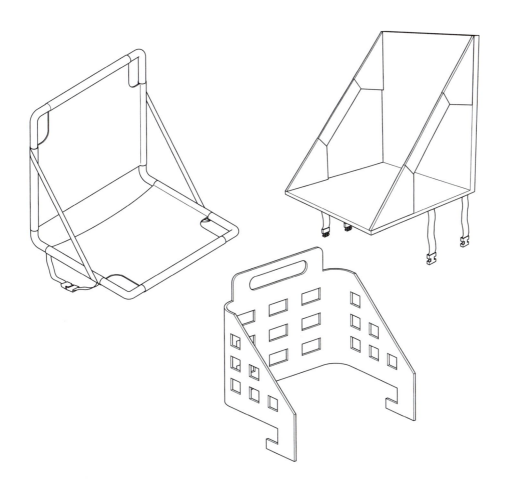

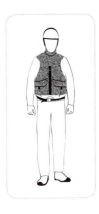

Figure 8.12
A variety of commercial canoe seat backs.

Folding lightweight fabric seat (canoe and kayak)

This seat, which has a soft foam core, provides back support but not side support. Some models can attach to the canoe or kayak seat (see figure 8.12). These more flexible seats fold when backward pressure is not maintained against them. Therefore, they are not recommended for paddlers who need any side support.

High seat back and lateral support for large paddlers (canoe)

If you need strong back support and fairly good side support for a large paddler, a handmade plywood seat back can be the solution (see figure 8.13). This seat back can be made from 1/2-inch (1.3 cm) or thicker plywood about 12 inches (30 cm) wide and 16 inches (41 cm) long or longer. The thickness depends on the paddler's size. The seat back should be about 14 inches (36 cm) to 18 inches (46) high and 18 inches (46 cm) to 22 inches (56 cm) wide. The seat back height should be equal to the height of the paddler's shoulders when sitting on a flat surface. The seat back width should be the width of the person's back 2 inches (5 cm) below the armpits plus 6 inches (15 cm). These additional 6 inches (15 cm) of width allow for 3-inch-wide by 5-inch-long (8 by 13 cm) foam wedges to be attached to the seat back to act as lateral supports for the paddler's torso.

If the paddler needs more lateral support than foam edges can provide, you can make plywood lateral supports. Also, plywood thigh supports can help position and stabilize the paddler's hips and legs. The lateral and thigh supports are attached to the seat back and bottom by corner irons and bolts. The seat back is attached to the seat bottom by a 12-inch × 1 1/2-inch (30 × 4 cm) piano hinge or two 2-inch (5 cm) hinges. These hinges should be made of a noncorrosive material such as stainless steel, brass, or aluminum.

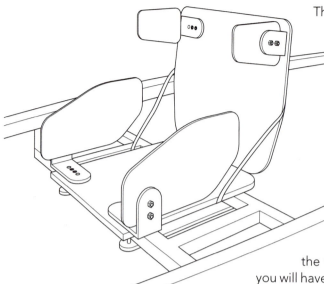

The seat back is kept upright by a 1/4-inch (0.6 cm), no-stretch, water-resistant cord that runs through holes in the seat back and bottom and then through a jam cleat on the front edge of the seat bottom.

Slide a piece of flexible PVC tubing over the cord on both sides to protect the paddler from abrasion. Usually the canoe seat will not provide enough seat depth to adequately support the foam seat wedge. Therefore, you will have to deepen the canoe seat. To build the additional seat support, select a 3/8-inch-thick (10 mm) or thicker piece of plywood depending on the paddler's weight and the necessary seat depth. The plywood should be about 12 inches (30 cm) wide and 16 inches (41 cm) long or longer for paddlers with long legs. The plywood can be attached to the canoe seat with carriage bolts clamped around the back edge of the seat (see figure 8.13). Once you have completed the seat back and deepened the seat with plywood, you can add the foam wedges and Ensolite layers, fine-tuning the outfitting as described in the section The Layering System on page 76 in chapter 7.

Figure 8.13
Wooden seat for a canoe.

Lowering a canoe seat

When extra cushioning and seat dump is needed as detailed in the Stable Seating section on page 70, you will need to lower the canoe seat to maintain trim. The goal is lowering the seat to get closer to the balance points designed by the canoe manufacturer; it will avoid a bell-buoy effect, which occurs when the seated paddler is too high after extensive seat adaptations. Remove the bolts and seat hangers (spacers between the seat and gunwale) (see figure 8.14a) and replace them with longer bolts and new seat hangers (see figure 8.14, b-c). You can make new seat hangers from 3/4-inch-diameter (2 cm) PVC pipe. Because the seat is actually hanging from the gunwales, provide more support under the seat with Ethafoam.

Figure 8.14
Lowering a canoe seat: (a) remove original canoe seat and hardware, (b) replace hanging hardware with longer bolts and 3/4-inch-diameter (2 cm) PVC pipe, and (c) reattach the seat with new hardware.

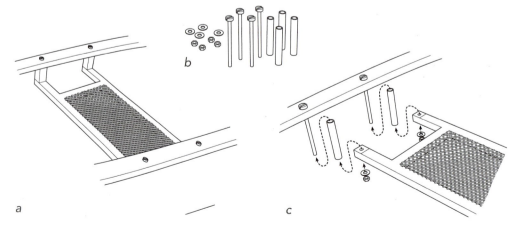

Adjustable seating systems (kayak and canoe)

Few after-market adjustable seating systems allow for increased stability for back and lateral support. Chosen Valley Creating Ability (CVCA) offers an adjustable seating system for canoes that clamps to existing bench-style canoe seats (see figure 8.15). The seating system provides seat cushioning and an adjustable seating angle/dump, and the back allows for several vertical adjustments to fit various torso lengths.

The CVCA universal paddling seat for kayaks has similar features, but it needs to be ordered specifically for the kayak in which it will be installed.

Figure 8.15
An adjustable seating system for canoes made by Chosen Valley Creating Ability (CVCA).

LOWER LIMB (LEG AND FOOT)

Commonly Related Conditions

hemiplegia, paraplegia, muscular dystrophy

Possible Implications for Paddling: Teaching Suggestions and Adaptations

See chapter 6 for additional advice concerning lower-limb impairments.

Seat support; difficulty sitting unsupported

Seating area adaptations

Use pieces of closed-cell foam and duct tape for seating area adaptations that give the paddler additional support. Placement of the foam pieces compensates for the person's lack of ability to brace against the boat with knees and feet. See the preceding section on neck or trunk impairments if the paddler needs more extensive adaptations to sit in a stable position.

Foam bulkhead

Installing a foam bulkhead in front of a paddler's feet can prevent a forward slide in the seat and help increase stability. See Building a Bulkhead on page 81 in chapter 7.

Difficulty maintaining boat balance

Lowering the seat

Drop the seat 2 to 4 inches (5 to 10 cm) to lower the paddler's center of gravity. In a kayak, this adaptation usually requires removing the existing seat and building a new seating system directly on the hull. (See the discussion of the kayak seating system on p. 72 in chapter 7.)

Ballast

You can create ballast inexpensively by using zip-lock bags or other containers filled with wet sand or various sizes of peanut butter jars. They can balance weight discrepancies in lower extremities due to muscle atrophy and help to achieve boat trim. The ballast contents cannot shift within the container because that movement would create instability. Weights designed for water workouts also make good ballast. Use your own experience to create inexpensive and adjustable types of stable ballast. Secure the ballast so it does not pose any entrapment danger for the paddler.

Decreased sensation and circulation; prone to skin abrasion and bruising

Patching of rough spots and seating area

Explore inside the kayak or canoe with your hands to find rough spots. Patch rough spots with foam and duct tape. Cover up the railings for the foot brace or foot pegs in a kayak. You can use pipe insulation and secure it with duct tape over the railing.

Seat padding

If the paddler has a history of skin breakdown, has had a surgical amputation, or has any other skin sensitivities, ensure that all boat parts that touch the skin are appropriately padded. Use Ensolite for cushioning. Neoprene provides minimal padding, but it helps cover up small, rough spots. It can also be used as a next-to-the-skin layer on top of Ensolite to provide extra traction in the seating area. (See the section The Layering System on p. 76 in chapter 7 for how-to details.) Do not use wheelchair cushions as part of boat adaptations. See the section Wheelchair Seat Cushions and Paddling on page 75 in chapter 7 for a discussion of the best options.

Commercial seats

Paddling stores carry a variety of seat pads designed specifically for use in a kayak or canoe. They are waterproof and easy to install on top of existing seats. Some simply provide an additional layer of padding, whereas others are contoured to provide better support in the seat. However, although these pads improve seating comfort, they may not provide sufficient padding for paddlers prone to skin breakdown.

Proper apparel

The use of proper paddling apparel can assist with skin protection. Neoprene pants provide a great layer of protection. However, they are inappropriate for paddlers whose body temperature control mechanisms have been disrupted, such as those who have had spinal cord injuries. Long pants made from nylon will help protect the lower extremities from mild skin abrasion.

Leg spasms or discomfort from overextension when seated in a kayak or on the canoe bottom; knee hyperextension; a tendency to slide forward in the seat

Knee rolls

Place a roll of non-water-absorbing foam 4 to 6 inches (10 to 15 cm) in diameter under the paddler's knees. Keeping the knees flexed tends to relax the muscles. A roll under the knees also helps to keep the paddler from sliding forward in the seat. Instead of just having one long roll of foam, you can use two short foam rolls, each about 6 to 8 inches (15 to 20 cm) long and placed under each knee. *Caution:* do not tape the knee roll to the boat. Be sure the roll(s) will not block easy exit from the kayak if a wet exit is necessary. Practice wet exits with the roll(s) in place and with nearby assistance. This adaptation is also helpful when a person sits in a seat on a canoe hull.

Feet slide out of place on the canoe bottom, causing the paddler to slide in the seat

Nonslip pad

Place a piece of material with a nonslip surface under the paddler's feet and glue or tape it in place. Place the paddler's feet on the material in a comfortable position. Because the feet rest on the nonslip material without any attachment to it, the paddler's feet simply fall away from the material in the event of a capsize.

LOWER-LIMB AMPUTATION

Possible Implications for Paddling: Teaching Suggestions and Adaptations

Difficulty bracing inside the boat as a result of a lower-limb amputation

Caution: Carefully evaluate the use of a lower-limb prosthesis while paddling. Even if the prosthesis is designed for water use, there is a high risk of entrapment in a closed boat when a lower-limb prosthesis becomes wedged during a wet exit. If the boat type poses an entrapment risk or the paddler's prosthesis is not designed for water use, develop an adaptation for the person when not wearing the prosthesis. Bring the prosthesis for use on land. Either keep it in a waterproof container secured in a boat during the trip or transport it inside a vehicle to the next takeout point. An above-the-knee prosthesis does not safely fit in a closed-deck boat with a paddler.

Foam bracing-point socket in a kayak for an above-the-knee amputation
Without the prosthesis on the residual limb, an adaptation must provide a contact point, or bracing-point socket, against which the paddler can press as he paddles to maximize boat control. Before creating this adaptation, ask the paddler to get into the kayak with the prosthetic sock or liner on and the prosthesis off. The prosthetic sock prevents socket-and-dirt abrasions, and more important, protects the residual limb in case the paddler ends up swimming. Neoprene shorts worn over the sock can provide additional protection. Using Ethafoam, shape a cupped bracing-point socket to fit the paddler's residual limb, padding it with Ensolite or neoprene to provide the needed cushioning for skin protection (see figure 8.16). Position this socket adaptation inside the kayak hull, and then duct tape it in place. If the paddler has bilateral amputations at the same level, both bracing-point adaptations can be contoured into an Ethafoam bulkhead.

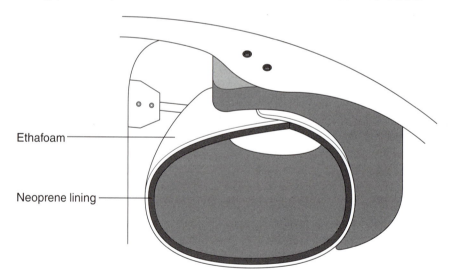

Ethafoam

Neoprene lining

Figure 8.16 Plastic socket attached to thigh brace for above-the-knee amputation (kayak).

Foam bracing-point socket in a kayak for a below-the-knee amputation
Create a bracing-point socket adaptation as detailed for an above-the-knee amputation and also use a foam knee roll to support the paddler's thigh, thereby maintaining a better angle for contact with the bracing point.

Plastic socket attached to thigh brace for above-the-knee amputation (kayak)
Caution: This adaptation requires some holes to be drilled in the kayak, so it is not appropriate for borrowed or rented boats. Above-the-knee amputees can be outfitted for closed-deck kayaks by using a plastic socket attached to the kayak's removable thigh

brace or a support structure. The paddler slides into the socket when entering the boat. This solution provides strong support—a stable brace—inside the kayak for paddlers who want to paddle more challenging whitewater or explore surf kayaking.

For the sockets you need a heavy-duty trash can or another source of 1/8-inch (3 mm) sturdy plastic, several flathead bolts (1 1/2 inches long, 3/16-inch diameter), 3/16-inch washers, 3/16-inch wing nuts, some Minicell foam, and duct tape. One trash barrel will make multiple sockets. Your main tool for this adaptation is a power drill with a 3/4-inch paddle bit or hole saw, a flathead bit, a Phillips head bit, and a 3/16-inch drill. In addition, you need a ripsaw, a box cutter, a Sharpie marker, a fine metal file, a Phillips head screwdriver, and a short-handled Phillips head screwdriver, which often comes with outfitting kits from boat retailers.

For an average-sized socket, cut a 24-inch-long (60 cm), 6-inch-high (15 cm) rainbow shape from the trash can by drawing the outline with a Sharpie and cutting it with the box cutter. Larger thighs will require larger sockets, and smaller thighs will require smaller sockets. Cut several of these strips for future use. Chip off the plastic burr and go over the rough edges on the plastic strip's long side quickly with a file.

To fit the socket, ask the paddler to get into the kayak with the prosthetic sock or liner on and the prosthesis off. The prosthetic sock prevents socket-and-dirt abrasions, and more important, protects the residual limb in case the paddler ends up swimming. Neoprene shorts worn over the sock can provide additional protection and improve the socket fit. Make sure to fit the socket when the paddler is wearing any additional clothing over the residual limb. Roll the plastic strip into a cone with the larger end pointing toward the paddler. Seat it comfortably and tightly around the residual limb, which should not be slipping through the narrow end of the plastic cone.

Let the paddler tell you what's firm and comfortable. If it is too close to the crotch, move it farther away, tighten the cone, and if necessary, cut a slimmer plastic strip. Mark the overlap with a Sharpie, pull the socket off, and lightly duct tape it together. Refit the socket. Ensure that the paddler can easily pull out of it. Adjust if necessary. If it fits, adjust the paddler's backband and hip padding; then adjust the thigh brace so the front of the socket is at the front of the thigh brace. Mark the final placement of the thigh brace. Remove the socket and the thigh brace. Save the bolts and nuts; they wander off if unattended!

Using the paddle bit or hole saw, drill two access holes down through the top part of the thigh brace—with one hole positioned toward the paddler and one toward the bow. Go easy and drill only through the top layer; don't go through to the bottom layer. You may choose to pull the protective stretchy cloth aside before drilling, or just plow through it. Once you have drilled each access hole, hold the socket under the brace, making sure the wide end of the socket faces toward the paddler. Drill a 3/16-inch hole through each access hole into the brace's bottom layer and through the socket.

Fasten the socket to the brace by sticking a flathead bolt up through the socket into the brace. Use the short Phillips head screwdriver to anchor the bolt and secure it by screwing the wing nut down on the bolt through the access hole. Do this for each access hole. Cover the screw heads in the socket with either duct tape or 1/16-inch (2 mm) foam.

Reattach the thigh brace to the cockpit. Check the fit. The paddler's residual limb(s) should be angled slightly toward the boat sides and upward. When seated in the socket, the paddler's residual limb and the bottom of the socket should be in line. The front of the socket is tilted downward slightly. Sometimes the socket needs to be lowered farther for the paddler to achieve a comfortable position. Using longer flathead bolts will allow for an adjustment with foam, plastic, or wood wedges between the thigh brace and socket. To keep the socket from moving too much, you can carve a foam wedge to fit between the socket and the boat floor and boat wall. Don't glue the foam to the socket or boat, because it will make it difficult to remove the thigh brace.

Lining the socket with neoprene or a thin foam layer can create a snug fit if a paddler decides not to wear neoprene shorts and the socket becomes too loose. The flexibility of this design is that you are outfitting a brace for a person rather than a whole boat. The person can take the brace with him and use it in other compatible boats, and the boat can be used for multiple paddlers.

Bilateral above-the-knee amputees can be outfitted by creating two sockets attached to thigh braces as described earlier. Another option is to use a supporting crossbeam (2- × 4-inch wood), spanning from one thigh brace to the other to which the sockets are attached (see figure 8.17). Once you have created the sockets, secure them to the crossbeam with screws. The crossbeam can either be attached to the boat in place of the thigh braces or screwed through the thigh braces if they cannot be removed.

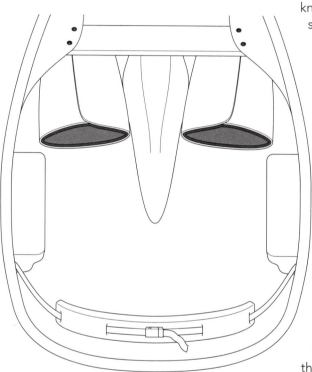

Caution: For bilateral below-the-knee amputees, the use of a cone-shaped, plastic socket can be dangerous because the leg can slip farther through the cone and trap the paddler inside the boat. The bracing-point socket created using Ethafoam is a safer adaptation for below-the-knee amputees.

Difficulty entering the canoe or kayak

Backrests (kayak)

In kayaks with adjustable backrests, lower the backrest into the reclining position. This incline enables the paddler to sit on the kayak deck behind the cockpit and then slip into the kayak from behind. *Caution:* Be sure that the deck behind the cockpit has been reinforced or is supported by a bulkhead or foam wall.

Figure 8.17
Double plastic socket.

Cockpit reinforcement (kayak)

If a paddler needs to sit on the kayak deck behind the cockpit to enter the boat, make sure the deck can support the person's weight in that location. The deck may already be reinforced with a bulkhead or foam wall. Otherwise, a support wall can be constructed using Ethafoam. (Minicell is too expensive for this use.) You can lean into the kayak and use picture wire to create a template for the shape of the support wall. Place a pad of neoprene on the deck behind the cockpit. The pad gives a nonslip and slightly padded area where a paddler can sit while positioning the legs in the cockpit and easing into the seat.

Possible Implications for Paddling: Teaching Suggestions and Adaptations

Unable to determine the position of the hands on the paddle shaft or the orientation of the paddle blade

Visual reminders

For a paddler who has limited sight, place small strips of tape just to the outside of the hand placement area on the paddle shaft (see figure 8.18). Using colorful electrical tape makes the reminders more noticeable; some folks even put the strips on either side of the hands to better show their proper placement.

Hand placement   Paddle orientation

Figure 8.18
Visual cues: *(a)* hand placement and *(b)* paddle orientation.

Indexing the paddle or blade angle indicator

People with visual impairments can identify the paddle blade orientation by feeling the shaft. On more expensive paddles, the paddle shaft is oval shaped in the grip area, which helps the paddler rotate the hand naturally into the correct position. You can create an even stronger indicator for blade orientation by attaching a short, straight stick, pencil, or chopstick to the shaft. First, identify the proper hand position on the paddle shaft and mark it. Put the index strip (chopstick) along the paddle shaft where the hand will be positioned and line it up with the center of the blade's back face. With two strips of tape, attach the index strip and check to make sure it is positioned correctly. When the hand grabs the paddle, the knuckles at the base of the fingers should line up with the top edge of the paddle blade, and the index strip should rest comfortably in the small space created under the next finger joints (see figure 8.19). If this is correct, use duct tape to secure the index strip in place.

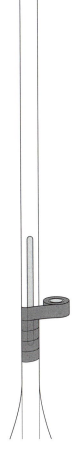

Figure 8.19
Indexing a paddle.

COGNITIVE AND BRAIN FUNCTION IMPAIRMENT

Paddlers who have a cognitive or brain function impairment as their primary functional loss may have a full range of secondary physical limitations as a result. In addition, functional losses may vary from a lack of quick reflexes to an inability to sit in one place for more than a few seconds unless that space is physically defined. The chapter 6 section on cognitive and brain function impairment (see p. 61) provides various instructional approaches. You can think about beneficial physical adaptations to the boat itself by studying the following sections in this chapter:

- Adapted seating systems (p. 91)
- Visual reminders (p. 101)
- Indexing the paddle (p. 101)
- Grip adaptations (p. 85)

9

Rescues

A primary concern during paddling programs and trips is participant safety. Knowledge and skill help to manage the risk in adventure sports, but the inherent dangers cannot be completely eliminated in canoeing and kayaking. As Laurie Gullion states in *Canoeing:* "Tipping over, an inevitable part of canoeing, can be caused by a paddler's losing balance, turbulent weather, or big wakes from other boating traffic" (Gullion, p. 64). All paddlers must be prepared to swim unexpectedly and understand self-rescue techniques.

Never paddle alone; your life may depend on aid from another paddler. Each rescue situation is unique and usually requires one or more rescue techniques. Assistance from a group will hasten the rescue, especially in cold weather and water.

Self-Rescue

The development of rescue skills is a necessary part of a student's experience because every rescue must begin with an effective self-rescue. When the boat capsizes, each paddler must be able to independently get out of the boat quickly and easily even if using adaptations. Everyone must also be able to independently turn faceup and make progress toward the shore. Do not participate in a paddling program if hands will be taped to paddles or people will be strapped to seats by any mechanism. Safe exiting is necessary for all paddlers.

Rescue Priorities

Early in the program all paddlers should wet exit (tip over) and practice rescue techniques appropriate to their abilities and the boats they will be paddling (see figure 9.1). All rescues must be practiced in a safe place (e.g., pool, quiet-water cove, or other protected area) where other people can stand and assist. Practice the rescues before you need to use them.

Practicing reentering the boat is essential. It allows students to experience what they most dread and to gain control by managing their rescue in a controlled environment. Practice also adds to the essential efficiency of the rescue. Rescues must be completed quickly to prevent immersion hypothermia because a paddler loses heat 32 times faster in water than in air.

03

Figure 9.1
(a) Wet exit in a
canoe, (b) wet exit in
a kayak, (c) reentry
using a scoop rescue,
(d) celebrating after
successful reentry.
Photo courtesy of
R. Mravetz.

The order of rescue priorities is the person first, then the boat, and finally the equipment. Before any outing, the trip leaders should decide and discuss with the group who will be responsible for which portions of a rescue. For example, if a paddler sees another paddler tip over, he should blow his whistle. At the sound of a whistle, paddlers should stop paddling, look around, and raft up (take hold of the gunwale of the closest boat) to prevent additional capsizes. The trip leader closest to the overturned boat will be in charge of the rescue and will call in others to assist as needed. Of course if the overturned paddler needs urgent assistance and you are the paddler closest to him, help him.

This section addresses rescues found to be effective with paddlers with disabilities and does not contain a general discussion of kayak and canoe rescues. It is important to consult a general guide to canoeing and kayaking for details on general rescue techniques (see appendix A, Resources). Ideally, a rescue class is very beneficial after introductory instruction and practice.

Scoop Rescue

Advantage

- This is the easiest technique for rescuing a person who has a weak upper body, has limited use of the legs, or is very tired.

Disadvantages

- This technique requires at least two other kayaks or canoes.
- It can be a slow process, so the paddler floats in the water for a long time.
- The boat is full of water when the paddler reenters it.
- The water has to be pumped out using a bilge pump—a slow process.
- It can be an unsafe method on a river, where the current may move the boats toward obstacles.

Process

1. The rescuer first takes the capsized paddler's paddle and secures it during the rescue.
2. The rescuer paddles beside the capsized kayak or canoe and turns the boat on its side with the cockpit facing away from the rescuer's boat.
3. The capsized paddler moves next to the overturned kayak or canoe, not between the two boats.
4. While on his back, the paddler guides his floating legs inside the cockpit of the overturned kayak or front of the canoe, then floats his body toward the front of the boat. If the paddler is unable to do so, assistance will be needed from a second swimming paddler.
5. When the buttocks are even with the boat seat, the paddlers holds on to the boat's upper edge with the hand that will be on that side when the boat is righted.
6. The paddler tells the rescuer that he is ready, and the rescuer pulls down on the boat's high side and rights it.
7. The paddler slides the rest of the way into the boat as it is righted. The rescuer supports the craft until the paddler is settled and balanced.
8. The boat is emptied using a bilge pump and other bailing aids (see figure 9.2).

Figure 9.2 Pumping out the water with a bilge pump.
Photo courtesy of R. Mravetz.

Boat-Over-Boat Rescue

Advantages

- This technique can be a fairly quick process, if the paddler has sufficient upper-body strength to reenter the kayak or canoe from the water.
- The boat is empty of water when the paddler reenters it.

Disadvantages

- The paddler has to have sufficient upper-body strength to reenter the boat from the water.

- The rescue requires at least one rescue boat (although two is optimum).
- The rescue is unsafe on a river, where a current may move the boats toward obstacles.

Process

1. The capsized paddler holds on to the paddle and the boat's upstream end (see figure 9.3*a*).
2. The rescuer approaches the capsized boat and grabs the other end of it. If a second rescue boat is assisting, it slides into position next to the first rescue boat to stabilize it (see figure 9.3*b*).
3. The swimmer can give the paddle to the rescuer.
4. The swimmer holds on to the end of the rescuer's boat as the rescuer pulls the upside-down craft up onto her boat (see figure 9.3*c*).
5. Water empties from the boat; a kayak can be rocked from end to end for more complete emptying.
6. The boat is then turned upright and placed next to the rescuer's boat in a catamaran (see figure 9.3*d*).
7. The rescuer helps the paddler get back into her boat by supporting it while reaching across and gripping the paddler's life jacket or waistband (see figure 9.3*e*).

Figure 9.3 Canoe-over-canoe rescue.

Towing an Upright Paddler in Flatwater

Advantage
- The assistance can allow a tired paddler to rest while the group continues to paddle (see figure 9.4).

Disadvantages
- The effort of the paddler who is towing the other boat increases.
- The person being towed may feel embarrassed.

Requirements
- A quick-release tow belt worn by the rescuer or a quick-release line attached to the rescuer's boat; the line is clipped to the paddler's grab loop.
- The towing paddler must be experienced in the technique.

Figure 9.4
A towed paddler.

Self-Rescue Swimming in Whitewater

Advantages
- The paddler assumes personal responsibility and acts immediately to self-rescue.
- The rescue can happen quickly.

Disadvantage
- The swimmer may not be able to see or hear a partner.
- Cold water can sap the swimmer's strength.

Process
1. The paddler immediately assumes a defensive position in the river, lying on his back with legs pointing downstream (see figure 9.5).
2. The paddler arches his back to stay as close to the water surface as possible and to avoid bumping his butt on the river bottom.
3. The feet stay near the surface. This tactic helps avoid one of the most common river hazards—foot entrapment, which is caused by standing in a swift current

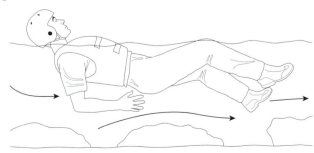

Figure 9.5
Self-rescue swimming.

and having the foot pushed into a crevice, snarled root, or tree limb. Paddlers should stand only when the water is knee-deep or shallower.

Rolling

Advantages

- The paddler does not exit the boat, so recovery is quick (see figure 9.6).
- The paddler's confidence is increased.

Disadvantages

- This rescue requires close instruction and considerable practice.
- This rescue is more difficult if the paddler does not have control of the hips and legs.

Requirements

- A positive attitude from the instructor and student is necessary because rolling can be a long, slow process.
- Kayak design is also important. Choose a comfortable, stable boat with a flat bottom and rounded sides for early practice to reduce frustration.
- Continue practice with the boat that the paddler usually uses.
- Check inside the boat for sharp edges, and remove the foot pegs if the paddler has limited use of the legs. Foot protection should be worn in the kayak (e.g., wet suit booties, sneakers).

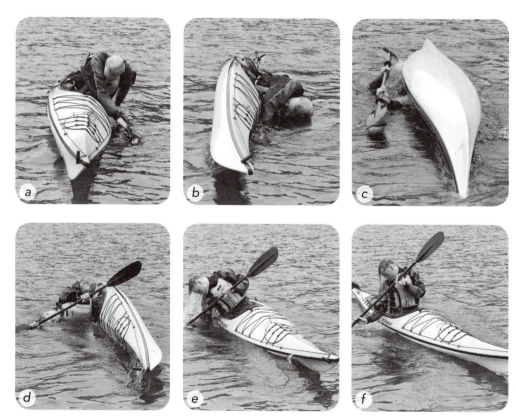

Figure 9.6
Rolling.

Adaptations for Rolling

In the process of rolling a boat, more important than hull shape is the outfitting that keeps paddlers in place in the seat. When the boat is rolled halfway over, paddlers without secure seating slide to the side or front of the boat, which may prevent completion of the roll. A tight neoprene skirt as well as a small-volume boat with padded knee and thigh braces will help hold paddlers in place during pool practice.

Rolling problems arise when people are so tight in the boat that they are unable to get free. Secure systems with small cockpits, thigh braces, and knee braces should be tried repeatedly in a safe environment such as a pool. At least three people should be with the paddler to right the boat in case of difficulty with exiting. Wet exits should always be practiced after any new adaptations are made. The paddler must practice using adapted seating systems and bracing systems until wet exits are quick and reliable.

Use of seat belts is very controversial because they can result in entrapment. Seat belts should not be used as an adaptation to the seating system even if the paddler usually uses a seat belt in a wheelchair. Instead, make other adjustments to the seating such as a change in angle and lateral supports. Never use self-adhering Velcro-type straps to restrain a paddler in a boat because that material can be difficult to detach when wet and can prevent from reattaching while underwater.

There is one exception to the rule of never using a seat belt for adaptations. Only in the following highly controlled and monitored situation when learning to roll in a pool setting is the use of a seat belt considered to be very cautiously acceptable. If a paddler who has loss of lower limb function found that they are unable to retain their position in the kayak seat when attempting to learn to roll, then a seat belt could be considered. Extreme caution and preparation are necessary for seat belt use during the process of learning to rolling. The paddler must practice wet exits and seat belt releases in a location such as a pool in a safe environment with calm, clear water and others to closely monitor and assist as needed. Only when the release is an easy, automatic response and the wet exit is quick should seat belt use be considered for general paddling. In case the release buckle fails, have at least one reliable backup system such as attaching the belt to the boat with a quick-release latch. The belt should be made of wide straps that pull over the student's lap and fasten with a large quick-release airline or jet-ski buckle with redundancy in the release both when the sprayskirt is pulled as well as manually.

For a person with limited leg control, put padding in the kayak between the legs so they do not fall to the kayak's low side when the boat tilts on its side. Duct tape a long tube padded with closed-cell foam on the boat bottom, which will keep the legs on either side of the kayak during a roll or while doing brace strokes. Make sure that the padding does not restrict the paddler from exiting the boat when it capsizes.

When teaching rolling in the pool, three instructors or helpers per craft increases the safety margin. The three people share the weight when lifting or righting the kayak, which decreases their risk of back injury. One person can stand next to the student, and the other two helpers can be positioned at the kayak ends on the opposite side from the first instructor.

Be careful when helping a capsized paddler back into the boat to avoid unnecessary injury to the person's skin and shoulders. The rescuer should avoid pulling upward on the paddler's arm and thereby injuring the paddler's shoulder(s) when righting the kayak with the shoulder lift. Instead, the rescuer should hold the paddler's arm, slide her other hand under the paddler's armpit, and push upward to lift the person. Encouraging the paddler to snap the hips to right the craft is also helpful.

Be aware that, with some disabilities, muscle spasms may occur when the person leans all the way back on the deck during a back deck roll. Wait until the spasms cease, and then proceed with the standard rolling instructional steps.

Another strategy is using a long paddle and an extended grip (hands offset to one end of the paddle). An offset grip allows the paddler to gain greater leverage from the additional paddle length. A paddle float may also add buoyancy to the working blade when bracing to roll up.

Reference

Gullion, Laurie. (1994). *Canoeing.* Champaign, IL: Human Kinetics.

10

Transfers and Carries

When a person needs some assistance, the focus should be on safety and dignity. Whether the need is moving from a wheelchair into a boat or crossing an area that is too difficult for a wheelchair, talking about and preplanning the process together are essential elements. This chapter provides the techniques for successful transfers and carries.

Transfers

A person transferring from a wheelchair to a boat may need help. That person is the expert on how to transfer from the wheelchair to another location. You know how the canoe or kayak will react when the person's weight encounters the boat and understand the safety issues involved. Talk through the transfer process with the person who uses the wheelchair to determine the safest and most respectful way to complete the transfer.

Because of the height difference between the wheelchair and the canoe or kayak seat, the person may need more assistance than he usually does when transferring. Transferring to a surface at a height midway between the wheelchair seat and the boat seat may make the total transfer easier. See the section Equipment on page 115 in this chapter for tips on midpoint transfer surfaces.

When assistance with a transfer is necessary, follow these steps:

Preparing to transfer.
Photo courtesy of J. Zeller.

1. Discuss all aspects of the transfer with the person who will be transferred before beginning. The top and tail method detailed on page 113 can be easily adapted to a wheelchair-to-boat transfer.
2. Planning is essential to ensure the person's safety and dignity.
3. Determine how the person will be picked up, especially appropriate hand placement to prevent any appliances from being dislodged.
4. When lifting, always bend at the knees, keeping the lower back straight, and using leg strength rather than back strength.
5. Use a spotter for each lifter in case the lifter loses balance.
6. Lifters and spotters should physically step through the planned transfer, walking and lowering an imaginary person into the final location, before picking up the person needing assistance.

7. Ensure that the wheelchair's brakes are locked.

8. After informing the person who is using the wheelchair, remove the armrest on the transfer side of the wheelchair. Spot the person on that side.

9. After a final check that the person is ready to be transferred, check that the other lifters and spotters are ready.

10. The lead lifter at the head counts to 3, and then all complete the lift and transfer.

Carries

Being carried can be a humiliating experience. It places the person in a childlike position of total dependence and draws the attention of onlookers. After a thorough review of all options, carries should be used only as a last resort in areas where the terrain is so difficult no other type of transport can be used.

When carrying the person is necessary, follow these steps:

1. From the beginning, involve the person who will be carried in the discussion.

2. Review all alternatives to carrying, including use of a wheelchair (see Tips for Crossing Beaches or Rough Terrain With a Wheelchair on p. 11 in chapter 3).

3. If no other solution is found, ask the person for permission to be carried.

4. Planning is essential to ensure the person's safety and dignity.

5. Discuss all details of the carry before beginning.

6. Determine how the person will be picked up, and discuss appropriate hand placement to prevent any appliances from being dislodged.

7. When lifting, always bend at the knees and keep the lower back straight, using leg strength rather than back strength to lift.

8. A spotter must be in place for each lifter and should be prepared to stabilize the person if a loss of balance occurs.

9. Lifters and spotters should physically step through the planned transfer, walking and lowering the person into the final location before picking up the person.

10. Ensure that the wheelchair's brakes are locked.

11. After informing the person who is using the wheelchair, remove the armrest on the transfer side of the wheelchair. Spot the person on that side.

12. Check with the person that she is ready to be lifted and carried, and check that the other lifters and spotters are also ready.

13. The lead lifter at the head counts to 3, and then all complete the lift and carry.

Transfer and Carry Techniques

The following information details the three most commonly used transfer and carry techniques and discusses the equipment that can be helpful.

Top and Tail Carry or Transfer

This technique is best with lifters of different heights because the carry causes an uneven weight distribution (see figure 10.1). The taller lifter at the head carries most of the weight. This technique is not recommended on uneven ground or over long distances. It is best for lifting off the floor or when transferring sideways.

1. *Top and Tail Transfers.* Follow steps 1 through 10 for Transfers listed on page 111, then add the 5 steps below. *Top and Tail Carries.* Follow steps 1 through 13 for Carries listed on page 112, then add the 5 steps below.

2. The person to be carried (the paddler) crosses her hands against her chest and grasps her own wrists.

3. The taller or stronger lifter stands behind the paddler, places his arms under those of the paddler, and grasps the paddler's forearms.

    o   The lifter squeezes his forearms against the paddler's sides, thereby keeping that person secure without straining the shoulders.

    o   The lifter's thumbs are placed on top of the paddler's forearms to avoid pinching the skin.

4. The second lifter at the legs can either lift from the side or from astride the paddler's legs depending on the setting. This lifter cradles the person's legs under the knees without pinching the skin.

5. The lifter at the head leads the lift and checks that the person being lifted is ready. When the person is ready, the lead lifter counts to 3, and then all complete the lift and transfer.

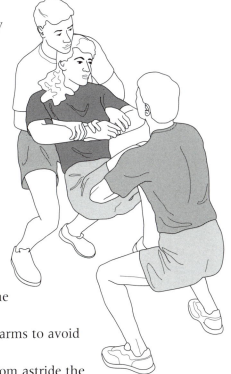

Figure 10.1
Top and tail carry.

Fireman's Carry

This carry is best to use when lifters are approximately the same height (see figure 10.2). It is useful for carries across longer distances and on uneven ground.

1. Follow the previous steps for transfers and carries. For transfers, use the preceding steps 1 through 10; for carries, use the preceding steps 1 through 13. Then add the following steps.

2. Each lifter places an arm around the lower back of the person to be carried.

3. The lifters place their other arm under the middle of the person's thighs. Their arms under the legs can be linked by a double forearm grasp or double wrist grasp.

Figure 10.2
Fireman's carry.

Stand and Pivot

The transfer technique is best when the person to be transferred can stand but cannot walk (see figure 10.3).

1. Follow the previous steps for transfers and carries. For transfers, use the preceding steps 1 through 10; for carries, use the preceding steps 1 through 13. Then add the following steps.

2. Set the surface from which you are moving as close as possible and at a 45-degree angle to the surface to which you are moving (the destination). For example, put the wheelchair as close as possible to the canoe.

3. Help the person move as far forward as possible in the wheelchair.

4. Help the person place both of his feet on the floor and lean forward. Be sure the person is wearing footwear with a non-skid bottom.

5. Stand directly in front of the person.

6. Bend at your knees and put one of your legs between the person's legs and one on the side of the destination.

7. Have the person give you a big hug around your shoulders without pulling on your neck.

8. Ask the person to turn his face toward the destination to see where he is going.

9. Tell the person you are going to stand up on the count of 3.

10. Count to 3 and pull the person forward from the hips into a standing position.

11. Slowly help the person take small pivot steps (small turning steps on flat feet) around toward the seat or destination.

12. When the person can touch the destination with the back of his legs, slowly guide him into a seated position.

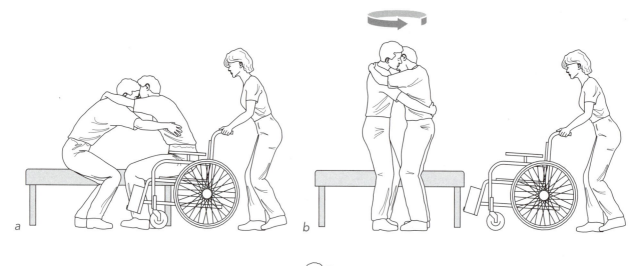

Figure 10.3
Stand and pivot
transfer.

Equipment

Certain equipment can help when transferring a person from a wheelchair to a boat. Because of the height difference between a wheelchair seat and a boat seat, you might consider using a midpoint transfer surface. When lifting, you may also want to consider wearing a back support to remind you to keep your back straight. Finally, a gait belt worn by the person being transferred gives those assisting her something to grab on to keep the person stable.

Midpoint Transfer Surfaces

An overturned plastic milk/storage crate or stool of a similar height is a handy portable surface. Place a thick piece of closed-cell foam on the overturned crate. When the person transfers to the midpoint surface, ensure that a lifter keeps their hands on the person to provide any needed stability for that person. Milk/storage crates can be purchased at most general merchandise stores.

Using a midpoint in transfer.
Photo courtesy of J. Zeller.

Back Support

Back support can consist of wide, elasticized bands with Velcro closures that encircle the waistline and lower rib cage. Wearing back support does not ensure against back injury; however, when properly worn, the back support serves as a powerful reminder to keep your back straight during the lifting process. Back supports are available for purchase at most of the larger home supply stores (for example, Lowe's, Home Depot) and online.

Gait Belt

A gait belt is a safety device placed around a person's waist to give those assisting him something to hold on to when moving him from one place to another. The belt is also used to help hold up a weak person while walking.

A gait belt is usually about 1 1/2 to 4 inches (4 to 10 cm) wide and 54 to 60 inches (137 to 152 cm) long. The belt is made of canvas, nylon, or leather and has a buckle at one end. Gait belts can be purchased at medical supply stores or online.

Follow these steps when using a gait belt:

1. Explain that the belt is used to prevent falls and will be removed after the transfer.

2. Thread the belt through the *teeth* of the buckle. Put the belt through the other two openings to lock it.

3. Be sure the belt is snug with just enough room to get your fingers under it.

4. When moving a person using a gait belt, prevent injuring your back by doing the following:

   ○ Bend your knees and keep your back straight.

   ○ Lift using your arm and leg muscles. Do not use your back muscles.

   ○ Keep your back straight. Do not twist your body while moving or lifting a person.

11

Paddling Trips

Paddling trips that include people with and without disabilities work well. The group shares a common goal of experiencing both paddling and nature apart from the usual routine of life. On both day and multiday trips, people must meet the challenges of the environment. Teamwork is essential on all trips, and each person's talents can add to the group experience. Individual respect is rightfully earned.

Planning is a must for all paddling trips, particularly those that combine people with and without disabilities. All participants must meet the essential eligibility criteria for the trip. All must also be told in advance that some participants will have disabilities. As the trip leader, you have to know exactly what assistance each participant will need. A detailed paddler's interview with each participant is essential to gathering that information. Plan for the equipment and any needed assistance for participants. Discuss disclosure if a participant's disability is not obvious but is likely to affect others or the group dynamics during the trip.

The sections that follow discuss things to consider when planning inclusive trips.

Paddling together.
Photo courtesy of Northeast Passage-NH.

Ratio of Paddlers With and Without Disabilities

The ratio of paddlers with and without disabilities depends on several factors, including each paddler's skill level and experience, the trip's length and difficulty, and the terrain at portages and campsites. The fact that a participant has a disability does not alone indicate the need for a higher ratio of paddlers without disabilities. A skilled and experienced paddler who has a disability might be a trip leader on the water and simply need some additional assistance carrying gear on a portage. However, a novice paddler with a severe disability may need more assistance on the water, especially on longer passages, during portages, and at the campsite.

The paddler's interview is the key to planning. Making a decision about the ratio comes from experience, but it is always better to have a few more experienced participants along than you think you need. However, proportion is essential; all trip participants should be expected to take an active part in paddling and group responsibilities at the campsites. An unbalanced ratio in the effort to ease the trip for those who have disabilities can result in overprotection that limits the participation of paddlers who have disabilities.

Route Selection

Scout all launching and landing sites, campsites, and portages before the trip. Make sure all participants will be able to move around the site and have access to the water and latrine. If independent access will be limited for people who use wheelchairs, walkers, and crutches, tell those participants before the trip and plan the type of assistance you will provide at those sites.

Taking Wheelchairs and Mobility Devices on Trips

Participant who use wheelchairs or other mobility aids such as canes, crutches, and walkers need to bring their devices on trips so they will have mobility on land. Many wheelchairs can be folded and placed in the center of a canoe bottom. Secure

Canoes hold a lot of cargo.
Photo courtesy of J. Zeller.

the wheelchair to the canoe (usually to a thwart) to prevent it from shifting during paddling and getting lost during a capsize. Practice rescues with the wheelchair tied in the canoe. Battery-powered wheelchairs are too heavy to be lifted and inappropriate for remote settings.

Most remote areas are not easily accessible to wheelchairs. In some paddling situations (e.g., a self-contained coastal kayaking trip with shoreline camping), it may be impractical to bring wheelchairs or other large mobility devices unless a canoe or other support craft can carry them. In those cases, a person who is unable to walk may have to accept being carried between the boat and the campsite and to the latrine. A person with upper-body strength can bring along cushions (e.g., a Jay Protector or boat cushion) to make it easier to scoot around on the ground. To lessen the feeling of dependence, a person with a disability can handle trip chores such as planning the logistics, creating menus, shopping for food and supplies, setting up tents, cooking meals, washing dishes, and packing common gear when breaking camp.

Wheelchairs and Mobility Devices on Portages

Many people who use wheelchairs can travel over the more level, well-cleared portages without difficulty. Uneven, rocky terrain or brushy trails are far more problematic. If there is any doubt about a participant's ability to manage a portage, you may want to make an assessment with the participant on similar terrain prior to the trip. For additional tips on crossing rough terrain with a wheelchair, see Tips for Crossing Beaches or Rough Terrain With a Wheelchair on page 11 in chapter 3.

Repair Kits

A participant who uses a wheelchair should bring the tire pump, patch kit, and wrenches that fit the chair. The wheelchair owner has this responsibility, but the trip leader should make sure these items are packed. If seating or other adaptations have been constructed, additional materials to make repairs may be needed.

Medications

Medications must be protected in waterproof containers. Participants should check with their pharmacists or doctors about proper storage. They should carry emergency medication such as bee sting kits in their boats. Each participant should carry a set of required medications, and a duplicate set should be stored in another boat.

Personal Hygiene

Provide nonembarrassing opportunities to go to the bathroom or latrine. A windscreen can be placed in front of the latrine if it is not located in a private place.

- *Accessible latrines.* The latrine needs to be accessible for anyone who uses a wheelchair. The pathway must be a minimum of 32 inches (81 cm) wide with a firm and stable surface. (See Accessibility at Launching and Landing Sites on p. 12 in chapter 3 for a discussion of stable surfaces.) A person using a wheelchair needs enough space to place the chair next to the latrine. That space must be a minimum of 32 inches (81 cm) wide by 48 inches (122 cm) long. A cleared 60-inch (152 cm) turning radius is needed in front of the latrine. Its seating height should be between 17 and 19 inches (42 and 48 cm) above the ground.

- *Folding commode seats.* Folding commode seats with legs that make the unit's seat height 17 to 19 inches (43 to 48 cm) above the ground can be carried with the trip gear and set up over a latrine that isn't the correct height. *Caution:* When using such folding devices, ensure that the equipment is appropriately set up, with adequate adjacent clear space, and is stable.

- *Alternatives to latrine.* If the group is using a portable latrine that is 17 to 19 inches (43 to 48 cm) high, set it up with adequate adjacent clear space in a very stable position with a side or backrest if possible. A tree can work well. At the very least, provide a person who has poor sitting balance with something to grab.

- *Raised toilet seat.* If you are sea kayaking or river boating and cannot transport a larger portable latrine, you can bring along a raised toilet seat, which is easy to assemble and dismantle for packing into small places. Use a unit with legs that make the seat height 17 to 19 inches (43 to 48 cm) above the ground. Place it over a previously dug hole in a location with enough clear space next to it that makes it easy for the individual with a disability to transfer onto it. This stable seat keeps the person off the ground.

Unfortunately, many people with spinal cord injuries or other disabilities must manage bowel and bladder routines, and they are often at a loss as to how to deal with these routines on long day or multiday trips. Here are some ideas that male and female paddlers with spinal cord injuries have used successfully:

- *Catheter/leg bags.* On long-distance paddling trips, catheter/leg bags may be emptied into wide-mouth quart-size poly bottles and dumped in a proper location.

- *Catheterization in a wheelchair.* People who do intermittent catheterization and take their wheelchair along can learn to catheterize themselves in their chairs.

- *Catheterization in a folding chair.* A very lightweight aluminum folding beach chair with a cloth seat, backrest, and no armrests can also be used as a place to catheterize. It sits about 4 inches (10 cm) above the ground and can be carried very easily on a sea kayak's back deck or lashed in a canoe. Its advantage is portability and allowing the person to urinate without exposing the skin to the ground. An added advantage is that the person can also use the folding chair as a comfortable camp chair.

- *Bowel routine without an accessible latrine.* When you cannot carry appropriate latrine equipment on the trip and when you have to carry out all human wastes, consider this routine: The person lies in a tent on his side on a large piece of heavy-weight aluminum foil to defecate. The entire package can then be wrapped up and placed in a zip-lock bag for later disposal.

Interviewing a Potential Outfitter, Guide, or Organization Before Taking a Trip

If you have a disability or you want to encourage a person who has a disability to get involved in paddling, there are some things to keep in mind. There are many opportunities and programs of varying quality around the country.

Here are the essential questions to ask:

- What training and experience has the outfitter, guide, or organization had in working with individuals with disabilities?

- What experience do they have working with disabilities similar to that of the specific individual who is considering the paddling opportunity?

- What are their safety practices for all participants?

- Are life jackets worn by all participants, including the instructors and/or trip leaders?

- If someone needs seating or paddle adaptations, how will those adaptations be provided? The person should be able to quickly and easily become free of those adaptations during a wet exit and should be able to do so without help.

- Do not participate if hands will be taped to paddles or if individuals will be strapped to seats by any mechanism. Safety is the key for all paddlers.

The outfitter's, guide's, or organization's responses to your questions will reveal their safety practices and their experience, including people who have disabilities in their trips. Their responses will also reveal if they view people who have disabilities as individuals with a wide range of abilities or as dependent, simply because they have a disability. Keep in mind that attitude and practices held by both the participant and the trip leaders can make or break a trip, so it is essential to ask these questions before deciding to sign up for the trip. Work with outfitters, guides, and organizations you feel you can trust and that will accept input from you. Be sure responsibilities and expectations are clearly defined in advance. Then be a full participant in the trip and broaden your paddling horizon.

Appendix A

Resources

Information on Paddling

- The American Canoe Association (ACA) Web site at www.americancanoe.org has information on canoeing and kayaking. You can also locate a course where you can learn to paddle and download brochures on safety and paddling instruction. Ask questions by sending an e-mail to sei@americancanoe.org.

- The International Scale of River Difficulty is on the American Whitewater Web site at www.americanwhitewater.org/content/Wiki/safety:start.

Information on Adaptive Paddling

- Information on training and certification in adaptive paddling is at www.americancanoe.org. Type "adaptive" in the search field for a list of options. You can find information on adaptive paddling workshops (APW), instructor certification for adaptive paddling equipment, and candidacy processes. Experienced paddlers who complete an APW will receive a certificate with an endorsement in adaptive paddling.

- Additional information about adaptive paddling is available at www.adaptivepaddling.org. Articles, resources, links, ACA adaptive paddling workshop listings, and contacts will put you directly in touch with ACA specialists in adaptive paddling equipment and instruction for canoeing and kayaking.

Accessibility

The U.S. Department of Justice ADA home page is at www.ada.gov. It has many resources and free publications on topics such as these:

- *The ADA Guide for Small Businesses*
- Service animals
- Tax incentives for improving accessibility
- ADA checklist for evaluating facility accessibility: www.ada.gov/racheck.pdf
- Current accessibility guidelines for facilities: www.access-board.gov

The U.S. Forest Service Web site at www.fs.usda.gov/recreation/accessibility features the laws and guidelines on accessibility and outdoor recreation.

- *Accessibility Guidebook for Outfitters and Guides Operating on Public Lands* is a 35-page document from the U.S. Forest Service on outdoor recreation–based businesses integrating people who have disabilities into all aspects of outdoor recreation, including the development of eligibility criteria.

- *Accessibility Guidebook on Outdoor Recreation and Trails* is a document from the U.S. Forest Service that contains information, illustrations, and URLs on integrating accessibility into the outdoor environment without changing the character and experience of the natural setting.

Disability-Related Organizations

Organizations related to other specific disabilities can be located through a Web search.

American Foundation for the Blind has resources for people who are blind or visually impaired: www.afb.org.

American Stroke Association is a division of the American Heart Association: www.strokeassociation.org.

Autism Society of America has resources on autism-related services and connections to local chapters: www.autism-society.org.

Independent Living USA provides a national directory of independent living centers in each state: www.ilusa.com.

Multiple Sclerosis Association has information and resources on this disease: www.msassociation.org.

National Center on Physical Activity and Disability is an information center concerned with physical activity and disability: www.ncpad.org.

National Spinal Cord Injury Association (NSCIA) has resources on a range of issues related to spinal cord injury: www.spinalcord.org.

Paralyzed Veterans of America (PVA) has information on veterans and spinal cord injury, publications, and connections to national service offices and local chapters: www.pva.org.

United Cerebral Palsy has information and URLs of additional resources: www.ucp.org.

Publications

- *New Mobility* is a magazine for active wheelchair users: www.newmobility.com.

- *Spinal Network* is book dealing with all aspects of disability for those who use wheelchairs. This book is available for purchase through *New Mobility* magazine's bookstore: www.newmobility.com/bookstore.cfm.

Organizations With Paddling Opportunities for People With Disabilities

The following are long-standing organizations nationally known for the quality of their work. Check the Internet and local resources for other opportunities. When considering paddling opportunities with an outfitter, guide, or organization, ask the safety and experience-based questions in chapter 11.

- Disabled Sports USA has the mission to provide the opportunity for people with disabilities to gain confidence and dignity through participation in sports, recreation, and related educational programs. They have chapters in every region of the country. Check the chapter listing for your state. Not all chapters have paddling opportunities: www.dsusa.org/about-overview.html.

- Northeast Passage (New Hampshire) is a nationally recognized sport and recreation program offering services in New England, including entry-level instruction, ongoing recreation in paddling, court sports, cycling, golf, hiking, water skiing, Nordic skiing, and power soccer with competitive opportunities in sled hockey and quad rugby: www.nepassage.org.

- Splore (Utah) specializes in promoting empowering experiences in an active, friendly world through affordable, customized inclusive recreation and education programs for people of all abilities in canoeing, rafting, and other sports: www.splore.org.

- Wilderness Inquiry (nationwide) has the mission to make outdoor adventure travel accessible to everyone regardless of age or disability through canoeing, sea kayaking, and rafting trips: www.wildernessinquiry.org.

Appendix B

Medical Information Sheet

Canoeing and kayaking are strenuous activities. If you have any questions regarding your health and participation in canoeing or kayaking, please discuss it with your physician. We ask you the following information to be aware of any potential problems and to help you enjoy the sport of canoeing or kayaking safely. Please use additional paper if necessary.

Name: _____

Address: _____

City / State / Zip: _____

Phone: _____ E-mail: _____

Height: _____ Weight: _____ Date of Birth or Age:_____

Section 1: General Questions

Describe your swimming ability: _____

_____

Describe your canoeing or kayaking experience: _____

_____

_____

Describe your general health: _____

_____

Section 2: Medical Information and History

Have you ever had any of the following? (please check the Yes or No column)

Condition	Yes	No	Condition	Yes	No
Allergies			Diabetes		
Heart disease			Asthma		
High blood pressure			Back problems		
Dislocations			Do you have muscle spasms? If yes, what triggers them?		
Do you get cold easily?			Are you greatly affected by heat?		
Are you pregnant?			Are you taking medication?		
Are you allergic to any medication?			If yes, are there any side effects of the medication such as sun sensitivity, increased thirst, or fatigue?		
Are you allergic to insect bites or bee stings? If yes, do you carry medication?			Seizures If yes, what triggers them? If yes, what is the date of your last seizure?		

(continued)

From J. Zeller, 2009, *Canoeing and Kayaking for People With Disabilities* (Champaign, IL: Human Kinetics).

Medical Information Sheet (continued)

If you answered yes to any of the questions in the chart, please explain here:

Condition

Symptom

_____   _____

_____   _____

_____   _____

_____   _____

Do you have a disability?   If yes, please describe:

_____   _____

_____   _____

_____   _____

_____   _____

How long have you had the disability? _____

Do you have a mobility impairment? If yes, please describe:

_____

_____

Do you have a sensory impairment (sight, sounds, or sensation)? If yes, please describe:

_____

_____

So that we can better understand your needs, please list any medical, physical, psychological, or emotional issues not mentioned above:

_____

_____

Insurance information

Company name: _____

Group / ID number: _____

Insured person's name: _____

In case of an emergency, whom should we contact?

Name: _____   Name: _____

Phone (day): _____   Phone (day): _____

Relation: _____   Relation: _____

From J. Zeller, 2009, *Canoeing and Kayaking for People With Disabilities* (Champaign, IL: Human Kinetics).

Appendix C

Paddler's Interview

Ask *every* student these key questions:

- What are your expectations?
- What type of paddling are you interested in—exercise, recreation, competition?
- Does your ability match that type of paddling?
- If not, are you aware of other paddling options such as sea kayaking and lake paddling?
- What are your concerns?

With the completed medical information sheet (MIS) in hand, do the following:

- Explain that the information on the MIS and gathered in this interview is confidential. The purpose is ensuring that you (the instructor) are prepared to help the student have a successful paddling experience.
- Ask if the student has any additional information to add to the form.
- Check whether there is any information that should be discussed.

Students need to understand that they are responsible for informing you about the extent of their abilities and skills. A comfortable conversation with the student will lead to more information exchange. During the paddler's interview, be sure to do much more listening than talking.

With the student who has a disability (if appropriate to the disability), do the following:

- Explain that you will be working together as a team. She is the expert on her disability, and you are the expert on paddling; working together, you both will succeed.
- Admit if you do not know about the type of disabling condition.
- Ask how long the student has had the disability.
- Ask questions about the disability or the management of symptoms *that are pertinent to paddling* (e.g., grasping the paddle).
- If the student has some loss of hand function, check on the ability to grasp the paddle by handing him or her a paddle.
- If the student has some loss of lower-limb function, check on sitting stability. Ask: "If you were seated on the edge of a bed and not holding on and someone pushed you firmly on your shoulder from the side, what would happen?"

- If the student has a visual impairment but has some sight, ask: "What can you see?"
- If the student has very limited vision or is blind, ask: "How do you generally learn how to do new things?" Similar methods might be applicable to paddling instruction.
- Ask whether the student anticipates any specific needs.
- Discuss disclosure—*if needed*—depending on the disability.

Explain the primary adaptation principle:

- You will use as much standard equipment as possible and will adapt equipment only as needed. You need the student's feedback on which adaptations or modifications are helpful and which are not.

To leave an opportunity for future disability-related questions, an appropriate ending question might be:

- "I think those are all the questions I have for now, but I may think of other questions later. If I do, may I ask you then?"

Appendix D

Skin: The Body's Biggest Organ System

The huge organ called the skin has unique characteristics that we all appreciate—primarily, that it keeps our insides inside. We give it care to keep it smooth and healthy. When we itch, we scratch it. When we've been sitting too long in one position, our brains automatically tell us to move to keep the blood following under our skin—that is, as long as our skin sensation is intact.

When a person loses skin sensation, which commonly occurs with a spinal cord injury, the brain connection doesn't function in the same way in areas of the body affected by paralysis. Automatic messages to move that assist in skin care no longer make it through, so skin care concerns and consciousness need to increase.

With paralysis, muscles shrink from lack of function, and the resulting atrophy means there is less cushioning between the bones and the skin. When parts of the body are pressed against a hard surface, the skin presses against the bone, and blood circulation is cut off. Without blood circulating, the skin cells begin to die. It takes only minutes for permanent skin damage to occur. The resulting skin breakdown, called pressure sores or decubitus ulcers, can take weeks or months to heal—and while healing, the person cannot put any pressure on that area. Surgery (skin grafts) may also be necessary, so the person may have to spend weeks or months on bed rest recuperating, which is a definite life-changing event.

Prevention is the key to skin care in paddling. Prevention measures include keeping skin dry, avoiding any points of abrasion, and ensuring that appropriate cushioning is always placed at potential pressure points. In paddling, the primary concern is seating because the pressure of body weight against the hard surface of the boat's seat, the pool's deck, or other hard surfaces forces bones into skin. It is essential to ensure that appropriate layers and densities of non-water-absorbing (closed-cell) foam are always between the person's bottom and the hard surface.

A person who has lower-limb paralysis needs to shift weight often enough to ensure that the blood keeps flowing under the skin. You may notice the person leaning from side to side or, if able, pressing down on the wheelchair sides to raise the buttocks up from the seat. In either case they are taking the pressure off long enough to get the blood flowing. This process is called pressure release.

In a boat the paddler may be able to lean forward enough to gain that release of pressure; if not, other techniques are available. In a tandem boat the paddler can let the partner know so the partner can steady the boat while she releases pressure. In a solo boat the paddler may need to raft up with another boat to gain the stability needed to lift slightly from the boat seat while pressing down on the cockpit rim or the gunwales.

Working together, you and the paddler can figure out the best ways to ensure a great paddle with no negative skin effects.

Appendix E

Spinal Column

A person with a spinal cord injury may be a paraplegic or a quadriplegic. When a spinal cord injury occurs, the level is designated (e.g., *C-4 quadriplegia*). Paraplegia results from injury at the T-1 (thoracic) level or below, and quadriplegia results from injury at the C-8 (cervical) level or above.

Neurological damage may be COMPLETE with no sensation or movement, or it may be INCOMPLETE with varying degrees of sensation or motion.

If the lesion is COMPLETE, the following applies:

- C-6 to C-8: impairment of hand and lower arm use. Some people may be able to grasp the paddle, but not have full hand motion.

- T-6: muscles below the nipple line are affected.

- T-8 and above: eliminates most balance while sitting.

- T-9 to T-12: eliminates abdominal muscles for rotating trunk and forward flexion of the trunk. Loss of some abdominal muscles also affects balance.

- Lumbar and sacral lesions affect leg muscles and torso, and balance remains intact.

If the lesion is INCOMPLETE, these effects will vary with the individual.

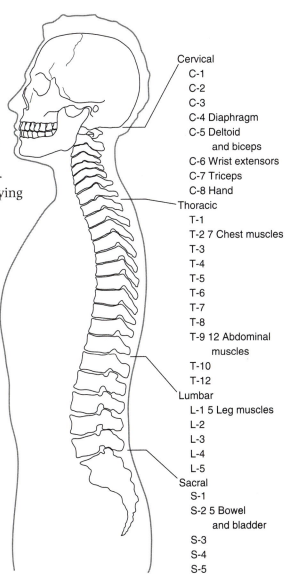

Cervical
C-1
C-2
C-3
C-4 Diaphragm
C-5 Deltoid
    and biceps
C-6 Wrist extensors
C-7 Triceps
C-8 Hand
Thoracic
T-1
T-2 7 Chest muscles
T-3
T-4
T-5
T-6
T-7
T-8
T-9 12 Abdominal
    muscles
T-10
T-12
Lumbar
L-1 5 Leg muscles
L-2
L-3
L-4
L-5
Sacral
S-1
S-2 5 Bowel
    and bladder
S-3
S-4
S-5

Appendix F

Universal River Signals

The signals in this appendix may be substituted with an alternative set of signals agreed on by the group.

Stop (potential hazard ahead). Wait for the *all clear* signal before proceeding, or scout ahead. Form a horizontal bar with your outstretched arms (see photo *a*). Those seeing the signal should pass it back to others in the party.

Help/emergency. Assist the signaler as quickly as possible. Give three long blasts on a police whistle while waving a paddle, helmet, or life vest over your head. If a whistle is not available, use the visual signal alone (see photos *b* and *c*). A whistle is best carried on a lanyard attached to your life vest.

All clear. Come ahead (in the absence of other directions, proceed down the center). Form a vertical bar with your paddle or one arm held high above your head (see photo *d*). The paddle blade should be turned flat for maximum visibility. To signal a direction or a preferred course through a rapid or around an obstruction, lower the previously vertical *all clear* by 45 degrees toward the side of the river that is the preferred route (see photo *e*). Never point toward the obstacle you want to avoid.

I'm okay (not hurt). While holding the elbow outward toward the side, repeatedly pat the top of your head (see photo *f*).

Glossary

Difficulties may arise when you are unfamiliar with the effects of a specific disability and how that disability may affect the student's paddling. Although it is important to have a basic understanding of potential limitations, you need not be a medical authority on every disease or condition before instructing people with physical disabilities. This brief glossary clarifies broadly the most common terms and conditions. The list is by no means exhaustive. However, some additional cautions and information have been added to some of the terms since the 1990 publication.

Although the Internet provides easy access to extensive information and you may wish to investigate there to learn more about a specific disability, keep in mind that each person is affected differently by a disability. Therefore, much of your extensive research may not be applicable to the paddler with whom you will be working. Remember: The person who has the disability is the expert on how that disability affects him or her. It is essential to look at each person's abilities relative to paddling, regardless of the diagnosis or condition.

amputee—A person who is without one or more limbs or a portion of a limb. The type of amputation is usually classified according to location. Depending on the location, amputations are referred to as follows: below elbow (BE) or above elbow (AE) as well as below the knee (BK) or above the knee (AK).

arthritis—An inflammatory condition involving the joints.

bilateral—Both sides of the body; frequently used to describe amputations to both sides of the body (e.g., a bilateral below-the-knee amputation).

catheter—A slender, hollow tube inserted into a body passage (e.g., into the bladder to draw off urine); it is connected to a collection container (leg bag) or used intermittently.

cerebral palsy—A nonprogressive condition occurring in the early stages of life (up to approximately two years of age), resulting in damage to certain parts of the brain with subsequent loss or impairment of muscle control and possibly sensation. There is a great deal of variation in the degree of involvement.

colostomy—The surgical creation of an opening for feces to pass through the abdominal wall.

decubitus ulcers—Pressure sores that are caused by sitting too long without proper padding, poor circulation, and so forth.

diabetes mellitus—A disease involving insulin deficiency and characterized by an excess of sugar in the blood and urine. Diabetes can be controlled with diet and medication in most cases.

epilepsy—Seizure disorder.

fatigue—Loss of strength or exhaustion. This is a frequent problem with many disabilities.

flaccid—Lacking muscle tone.

hearing impairment—A partial or complete loss of hearing.

hemiplegia—Some degree of impairment of the muscles and/or sensation in the arm and leg on one side of the body; may result in flaccid or spastic muscles.

lower extremities—Legs and feet.

lung disease—A chronic disorder involving the lungs or mechanics of breathing (e.g., asthma, emphysema, and neurological or muscle disorders impairing the respiratory muscles). Asthma is a chronic disease characterized by labored breathing or wheezing.

multiple sclerosis—A relapsing disease of the central nervous system affecting various parts of the body; may produce fatigue, weakness, poor balance, tremor, decreased sensation, and muscle paralysis.

muscle spasms—Sudden involuntary contractions of muscles or muscle groups; spasms may be painful. They may be triggered by sudden submersion in cold water, overexertion, or improper seating. Spasms cannot be controlled once they start; one must wait until the movement stops.

muscular dystrophy—A progressive disease resulting in a weakening of the muscles with decreased muscle tone; causes fatigue.

paraplegia—Some degree of paralysis or loss of sensation in both legs and possibly lower parts of the body; may result in muscle spasms in the legs. Paraplegia usually results from an injury or disease affecting the spinal cord from the T-1 level or below.

phlebitis—Inflammation in a vein. Thrombophlebitis is due to one or more blood clots in a vein that cause inflammation.

posttraumatic stress disorder (PTSD)—An anxiety disorder that can develop after exposure to a terrifying event or ordeal in which grave physical harm occurred or was threatened. Traumatic events that may trigger PTSD include violent personal assaults, natural or human-caused disasters, accidents, or military combat.

prosthesis—An artificial limb or artificial substitute for a missing body part.

psychotropic drugs—Drugs that affect the mental functions or behavior.

quadriplegia—Some degree of impairment of muscles or sensation with paralysis in all four limbs. Trunk stability may be affected. The person may have some use of the arms but reduced hand function and may experience muscle spasms. See the diagram and information on page 133 for more detail.

residual limb (stump)—The portion of the limb remaining after amputation.

sensation—The ability to feel sensory stimuli such as touch, pain, heat, or cold. Sensory loss may be total or partial.

spasticity—A condition in which hyperactive muscles move involuntarily. See *muscle spasms*.

spina bifida—A birth defect of spine and spinal cord; may result in weakness and loss of sensation or complete paralysis of the legs below the level of the defect on the spine. Bladder and bowel control may be affected; this will vary with the person.

spinal cord injury or disease—A spinal cord injury is damage to the spinal cord that causes loss of sensation and/or motor control. The resulting of loss of physical function is referred to by its level (e.g., a C-6 quadriplegic has injury at the sixth cervical vertebra).

transfer—Movement from one surface to another; usually refers to moving to or from a wheelchair (e.g., moving from a wheelchair to a boat).

traumatic brain injury (TBI)—Also called acquired brain injury or simply head injury, it occurs when a sudden trauma causes damage to the brain. Functional losses resulting from a TBI depend on the severity of the injury, the location of the injury, and the age and general health of the person.

tremor—An involuntary trembling movement; often seen in people with multiple sclerosis and Parkinson's disease.

trunk stability; balance in sitting—Trunk muscles that allow a person to stand or sit unsupported are weakened or absent in some conditions. Therefore, the person is unable to balance without support.

upper extremities—Arms and hands.

visual impairment—The loss of some ability to see, either partially or completely. Many people with visual impairment have some sight. Some people see lines, shapes, or colors; others can detect only light and shadow.

Note: The italicized f and t following page numbers refer to figures and tables, respectively.

About the Author

Janet Zeller is a lifelong paddler. She has participated in numerous wilderness and whitewater canoe trips, and since 1982 she has also been a sea kayaker. After a 1984 accident resulted in quadriplegia, she was determined to return to paddling, so she looked for opportunities but found there weren't many. She gathered expertise, encouraged development, and coordinated resources for adaptive paddling opportunities. Janet is still passionate about both paddling and the wilderness and goes paddling every chance she gets.

In 1989 Janet approached the American Canoe Association (ACA) and shared the need to develop opportunities for people with disabilities to experience paddling. The ACA endorsed the effort, and she formed the adaptive paddling program. In 1990 Janet coauthored the book *Canoeing and Kayaking for Persons With Physical Disabilities.*

Janet also worked with others to develop the ACA's Adaptive Paddling Workshops (APWs) to train canoeing and kayaking instructors, therapists, and those who run water-based recreation programs in the techniques for integrating people with disabilities into their programs. Janet is an ACA instructor trainer educator, instructs APWs across the country, and has mentored others in becoming APW instructors for those sessions. Since the APWs began in 1990, hundreds of instructors and program managers have participated, opening paddling opportunities to countless people with disabilities as well as to their families and friends.

Employed as the national accessibility program manager for the U.S. Forest Service, Janet works with the 175 national forests and grasslands across the United States. She also represents the Forest Service in her work with organizations and other federal agencies.

Janet has authored numerous articles and is an instructor and speaker on accessibility, universal design, and inclusive outdoor recreation at national, regional, university, and local forums. She has a bachelor's degree from the University of New Hampshire and a master's degree from the University of Rhode Island.

About the Editor

Laurie Gullion got hooked on remote Canadian rivers in 1980 with a 1,000-mile trip on the Elk, Thelon, Dubawnt, Kunwak, and Kazan rivers in the Northwest Territories. She has since canoed more than 12,000 miles in Alaska, Canada, Norway, and Finland—always in search of Arctic and subarctic wildflowers, large mammals, and routes that take her to less-traveled rivers.

Author of the American Canoe Association's *Canoeing and Kayaking Instruction Manual* (1987), Laurie has published seven books on canoeing, kayaking, and Nordic skiing. Her *Ragged Mountain Press Woman's Guide: Canoeing* includes stories from women who have paddled more than 60 years. She is currently collecting information on women who traveled by canoe or kayak from 1850 to the 1940s. Since few women published accounts of their travels, she is searching in journals, letters, and scrapbooks for tales of women who paddled on lakes and rivers in North America.

Laurie coordinates the undergraduate option in outdoor education at the University of New Hampshire at Durham, where she trains outdoor educators to lead a variety of adventure programs. The put-in for sea kayaking trips is five minutes from her office on the largest inland estuary in the Northeast. She contributed the canoeing curriculum in *Technical Skills for Adventure Programming* (2009) and has been certifying ACA whitewater canoeing instructors for more than 25 years.

Please contact Laurie at lgullion@unh.edu with any historical information that you have on women and canoeing.

About the Contributors

Colin Twitchell is the founding director of the Lemelson Assistive Technology Development Center and teaches applied design, invention, and entrepreneurship at Hampshire College in Amherst, Massachusetts. Colin developed the adaptation principles and processes used in the adaptive paddling program and has been an ACA instructor trainer educator in adaptive paddling equipment. Colin's entrepreneurial and design work includes development of several types of adaptive recreational equipment, the start-up of several businesses, and work with international organizations in the development of adaptive equipment. His designs have been exhibited at the Smithsonian National Museum of American History and the United Nations.

Sybille Fleischmann discovered her love of paddling as a child with her mother on the Donau River in Germany. She has been working with the ACA adaptive paddling program since 2003, organizing workshops for instructors and teaching in kayak schools, rehabilitation centers, and outdoor programs across the United States. Based in the Pacific Northwest, Sybille supports local initiatives to make paddling more accessible to everyone and also manages adaptivepaddling.org, an online forum for paddlers with disabilities. She is an ACA instructor in adaptive paddling equipment, coastal kayaking, and whitewater kayaking. When she isn't paddling, Sybille works on initiatives to deliver technology to underserved communities in her capacity as a product planner for an information technology company.

Jeremy Oyen is the American Canoe Association director of safety education and instruction. He has worked in the paddlesport and outdoor education field for over 20 years, serving as a wilderness canoe guide, canoe and kayak instructor, manager of an outdoor specialty store, paddlesport buyer, owner of Lake Erie's first sea kayak guide company, and manager of Cleveland Metroparks nationally recognized Institute of the Great Outdoors, where he received the International Boating Education and Advancement Award for their inclusive paddlesport program. Jeremy holds a teaching license in secondary education. He is also an ACA instructor trainer in adaptive paddling equipment and coastal kayaking and instructor in canoe touring, river canoeing, and river kayaking.

Scott LeBlanc is a certified therapeutic recreation specialist (CTRS). Since 1991, he has worked in physical rehabilitation hospitals, directed adapted sport and recreation programs, and taught at the collegiate level. Scott is a consultant and speaker on inclusion, accessibility, and access to recreational opportunities for all. Beginning as Colin Twitchell's student in the early 1990s, Scott has continued the development of adaptive equipment design and technique in paddlesports. Scott is an ACA instructor trainer educator in adaptive paddling equipment and an instructor in essentials of river kayaking and essentials of kayak touring.

Additional Contributors

M. Jan Tackett, PhD, staff psychologist, Veterans Administration Puget Sound Health Care System

Dave Robey, Team River Runner, volunteer

Lynne Warner, Team River Runner, San Diego volunteer

Elaine Mravetz, ACA instructor trainer and former special education teacher and consultant

April Rosenthal, ACA instructor and certified recreation therapist

Nancy Uschold, ACA instructor and physical therapist

Crystal Skahan, MS, ACA instructor and licensed recreation therapist

Sam Crowley, ACA instructor trainer educator and sport massage therapist

About the Organization

The **American Canoe Association (ACA),** founded in 1880, actively promotes paddlesports across the United States, providing programs and services to its members and the American public. The ACA has these objectives:

Make paddling education and instruction accessible to the public.

Improve access to paddling for current paddlers and provide avenues for casual paddlers to become paddlesport enthusiasts.

Expand paddlesport into the underserved and high-need segments of the market.

Influence issues and public policy that affect paddlers and the paddling experience.

Create strategic alliances with the other organizations that represent the outdoor experience in order to expand awareness and knowledge of paddling concerns.

ACA members are a great resource for carrying the ACA mission forward. It is important for the ACA to provide guidance, leadership, and information on furthering its educational, stewardship, and recreation tenets at the local, regional, and national levels.

Recognized as the gold standard for paddlesport safety education and instruction, the ACA is uniquely qualified to help individuals and organizations understand how paddlesports can contribute to the quality of life through enabling safe and positive paddling experiences.

The ACA strives to communicate the benefits of canoeing, kayaking, and rafting as lifetime recreation and keeps participants informed about paddlesport opportunities and activities, thus helping to advance the sport. Focus of the organization's work is on four strategic tenets: education, competition, stewardship, and recreation.

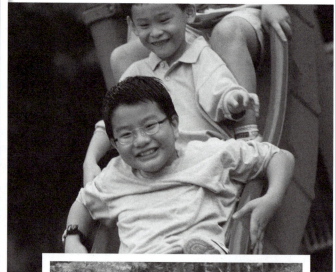

You'll find other outstanding
recreation resources at
www.HumanKinetics.com

In the U.S. call 1.800.747.4457
Australia 08 8372 0999
Canada. 1.800.465.7301
Europe . . . . .+44 (O) 113 255 5665
New Zealand . . . 0064 9 448 1207

HUMAN KINETICS
The Information Leader in Physical Activity
P.O. Box 5076 • Champaign, IL 61825-5076